MONTGOMERY INK BITES COOKBOOK

MONTGOMERY *Ink Bites* COOKBOOK

SHORT STORIES BY *NEW YORK TIMES* BESTSELLING AUTHOR

CARRIE ANN RYAN

RECIPES FROM *USA TODAY* BESTSELLING AUTHOR

SUZANNE M. JOHNSON

BLUE BOX PRESS

MONTGOMERY INK BITES COOKBOOK

Short stories copyright 2022 Carrie Ann Ryan
Recipes copyright 2022 Suzanne McCollum Johnson

ISBN: 978-1-952457-93-7

Published by Blue Box Press, an imprint of Evil Eye Concepts, Incorporated
All rights reserved. No part of this book may be reproduced, scanned, or distributed in any printed or electronic form without permission. Please do not participate in or encourage piracy of copyrighted materials in violation of the author's rights.

This is a work of fiction. Names, places, characters and incidents are the product of the author's imagination and are fictitious. Any resemblance to actual persons, living or dead, events or establishments is solely coincidental.

Foreword

I've always been a foodie. In fact, before I wanted to be a chemist and one day a writer, I wanted to be a chef. My father taught me to cook, and I'd always imagined myself cooking in a lovely kitchen, making up all new recipes.

When I started writing, I loved incorporating food into each of my books. My characters would cook, eat, and appreciate their food. So much so, in fact, my editors all joked that I needed to warn them what to eat ahead of time!

Doing this project meant the world to me because I got to work with an amazing chef to figure out exactly what these Montgomerys would want to make! Writing the stories of the original Montgomerys brought me back and I'm so glad I got to visit some of my favorite characters and write yummy dishes in each set!

In this cookbook, you'll meet each of the original Montgomerys and the families they've made over time and see how food is important to them as well as me. Not only this, but it prepares you for the next generation of Montgomerys in the Montgomery Ink Legacy series since more romances are on the way.

Thank you so much, Suzanne, for working with me on this. I so loved working with you and Liz on this amazing project!

Happy reading and eating, dear readers!

Table of Contents

CHAPTER 1: Just a Bite 1
Zesty Meatballs 12

Jarcuterie Cups 13

Dirty Martini Deviled Eggs 14

Loaded Potato Dip 14

Blue Cheese Chicken Bites 15

Smoked Maple Bacon 15

CHAPTER 2: Bring on the Temptations 17
Cajun Chicken Pasta Alfredo 26

Whiskey Honey Ribs 27

Orange Chicken 28

French Dip Au Jus 29

Bold Burger 30

CHAPTER 3: Spice it Up! 31
Buffalo Chicken Stuffed Bread 40

Peach Pepper Jelly Grilled Chicken 41

Spicy Corn Chowder 42

Beef Curry Stir Fry 43

Memphis Chicken 44

CHAPTER 4: All About the Veggies 45

Veggie Lasagna 52
Tuscan Portobellos 53
Southwest Pasta Salad 54
Green Goddess Salad 54

CHAPTER 5: With a Twist 55

Cheeseburger Spring Rolls 64
Reuben Quesadillas 65
Chili Cheese Waffles 66
Spicy Pop Tarts 68
Cheesesteak Stuffed Peppers 69
Eggroll Lettuce Wraps 70

CHAPTER 6: Cheese Me, Baby 71

Cheesy Chicken Enchiladas 80
French Toast Grilled Cheese with Bacon 81
3-Cheese Hashbrown Casserole 82
Fried Cheese Curds 82
Broccoli Cheese Soup 83
Steak and Cheddar Melt 84

CHAPTER 7: Call Me Cupcake 85

PB&C Cupcakes (Peanut Butter & Chocolate) 94
Tiramisu Cupcakes 95
Banana Split Cupcakes 96
Peaches and Cream Cupcakes 97
Steak & Ale Pie 98

CHAPTER 8: Isn't It Sweet...99

S'mores Cinnamon Rolls 108

Gooey Butter Cake 109

Butterfinger Pie 109

Chocolate Bread Pudding 110

Raspberry Dark Chocolate Fudge 110

Caramel Pecan Clusters 111

Index.. 112

Also From Carrie Ann Ryan 114

About Carrie Ann Ryan 119

Connect with Carrie Ann Ryan 119

Also From Suzanne M. Johnson 120

About Suzanne M. Johnson 121

Connect with Suzanne M. Johnson.. 121

CHAPTER 1

Just a Bite

Austin

My kid wasn't supposed to be graduating from high school. How was that even possible? Wasn't he just some ten-year-old sitting on my step wondering what the hell was going to happen next?

I shook my head and leaned against the doorway as I watched Leif and Sierra pack for the trip.

"Are you going to keep getting so emotional, Dad?" Leif asked, pushing his hair from his face. He'd decided to go with some new age teenager haircut that had his hair way too long in the front, and he looked like some boy bander that I didn't understand. He also used lingo that I kept having to ask what it meant. I had to wonder when the word 'cool' wasn't so cool anymore. Nothing reminded you that time changed and you were getting old like a teenage boy in your house.

"I'm not getting all reminiscent over some shit," I growled, glaring at Leif.

My wife laughed, tossing her mane of hair back over her shoulder. "You are getting a bit growly. And I thought it was my job to get all emotional and weepy over the fact that our baby boy is getting all grown up and about to be an adult in the real world. Soon you're going to have to wash your own underwear routinely and everything."

She went to her tiptoes and messed up Leif's hair. Our son just rolled his eyes and then proceeded to mess up his hair even more. Or maybe he was just putting it back into some form of style. It wasn't like I was a master in style. I had never been. I was a tattoo artist who tended to forget to get a haircut until I buzzed it all off. I always kept my beard, though, since Sierra loved it.

But the kid had a way with the girls at school, so maybe he was on trend when it came to his wild hair.

"I wash my own underwear," Leif growled, his cheeks reddening. "And seriously, Mom, you taught me how to do laundry when I was like thirteen."

Sierra beamed at the use of the word "mom." It didn't matter that it had been nearly eight years with Leif in our lives, that my son had shown up right around the time that I had fallen for the love of my life. It still felt new, as if we were figuring out who we were together.

Leif had come into my life when everything had changed, and I couldn't be prouder of the kid. He'd lost almost everything, and I hadn't even known he had existed until he had just shown up, and now that he was here, our lives were completely different.

He had started calling Sierra "Mom" after the wedding, and even more often after the formal adoption papers had been signed. Sierra was his mom, and I was his dad, even though I hadn't been there the first ten years of his life. But I wasn't going to lose any more time.

This weekend would be all about Leif and making sure he got to visit the schools that he could potentially go to around Colorado and up into Wyoming. Later, we'd be traveling to California, Oregon, and Washington to look at some out-of-state schools. My bank account whimpered at that thought, but if Leif wanted to go to school out of state, then we would find a way. We always did.

"Okay, I think we're mostly packed," Sierra said as she patted the suitcase. "And remember, I taught you how to do laundry and make your own food when you were younger. So you can take care of yourself and not have to eat ramen and wear dirty underwear for the rest of your life."

"I would just go without underwear, duh." Leif rolled his eyes as Colin ran into the bedroom and jumped on Leif's bed.

Colin was five years old and could do somersaults off the thing like he was a pro gymnast. It was honestly a little scary, and when Colin proceeded to do just that, both Sierra and I held out our arms, trying to catch him, but Leif was the one who did with a wide grin.

They looked so much alike. It was a little startling to see how much of the Montgomery genes were in both of them. Leif tossed Colin over his shoulder, upside down, and my youngest son just giggled, kicking his feet up in the air.

"What did we say about jumping on the bed?" Sierra asked, tapping her foot. I held back a grin, trying not to indulge either one of them. Leif set Colin down, and my youngest ran smack into my legs. I ran my hand over his soft hair, noticing that it was getting a little darker over time. He had been born a towhead and was slowly getting that dark chestnut that was all Montgomery.

My heart ached at remembering wanting a little girl or boy with Sierra's eyes, knowing that would never happen. We had tried, and I'd almost lost my wife. We wouldn't be trying again, and the dream of more children, for the big family that we had both always wanted, wasn't going to happen.

We had been on adoption lists for years now and hadn't been chosen by a birth mom. We'd had trouble with the foster system because of my job and the fact that our kids were so far apart.

Things just hadn't worked out for us, but we were a family of four, and we were making it work.

"Sorry!" Colin beamed, not looking sorry in the least. I had once thought living with a teenager was tough to handle, as Leif had his own issues even if he was a pretty decent kid. A five-year-old was even worse. Somehow, Colin had both mine and Sierra's hyper-tendencies all rolled into one, even though the kid tried his best to be good. He was a sweet kid, without a mean bone in his body, but.

"I get to go, too, right?" Colin asked.

Leif was the one who answered. "Of course. You're going to have to help me figure out the school I want to go to."

"But you won't be gone for too long, right? You'll still be close? I don't want you to go." Colin's teeth worried his lip, and I met Sierra's gaze, knowing Colin was just as nervous about Leif leaving the house as we were.

Our family was a big one. I had seven siblings, and most of my siblings had at least two kids. Griffin and Autumn had decided to be the legendary aunt and uncle rather than parents, and their choice was exactly perfect for them. Because there were so many cousins, it sometimes felt like a never-ending run of kids. However, Leif was the oldest by far. Only one of my cousins' kids was near his age. Everyone else was a good ten years or so younger.

Meaning I was the first one sending my kid to college, while the rest of my siblings were still procreating.

It was an odd jump, and that meant that we didn't know what we were doing yet, and Colin wasn't ready to say goodbye to his brother.

Leif hugged Colin close and sighed. "It'll be okay. I'm probably going to stay in-state anyway. It'll be cheaper for Mom and Dad, and I'll be close to you."

Colin sighed into his brother as I met my wife's eyes at Leif's words. "That means we get to do brother things?"

"Of course."

Leif hugged Colin tight, and Sierra moved towards me, sliding her hand into mine.

"We did good," Sierra whispered.

"We still are." I kissed the top of her head and looked down at my phone. "And we need to start working on dinner so that way we can head to bed early."

3

"Yes, because we are leaving for our trip." Sierra clapped her hands. "Should be exciting."

"Okay, I want to help!" Colin wiggled out of Leif's hold and ran out of the room, Leif following him with a smile playing on his face.

I tugged on Sierra, bringing her close as I lowered my lips to hers.

"We're doing okay, right?" she whispered.

"Of course, we're doing okay. Our kids are healthy—God willing—smart, a little mischievous, but they're Montgomerys. It's what we do."

"They *really* are Montgomerys, through and through. I still can't believe our oldest boy is ready to leave the nest. And leave us."

I sighed at her words. "Hey, it looks like he wants to stay close. That's good, right?"

Sierra winced. "I know it's expensive for him to go out of state, but he's smart enough to get scholarships, and we're working hard on it. I don't know. It's just odd to have to limit him this way."

"Hey, Colorado schools are great. We'll find a way to make it work."

"I know, I just know that Colin wants him to stay here."

I raised a brow. "And what about us? We're not pushing him out of the nest, are we?"

"No, but our baby's growing up."

I held her close, then kissed her softly, the kiss deepening.

"Stop making out in my room!" Leif growled. "If I'm not allowed to bring girls in here, you're not allowed to make out with Mom."

"Yes. Right!" Colin added, and I laughed against my wife's lips, tugging her out of the bedroom and into the kitchen.

"He's got a point there," Sierra said primly, her eyes sparkling.

I rolled my eyes. "Maybe. But we don't have to let him know he has a point."

"True."

"Okay, what are we doing for dinner again?"

"We decided on an appetizer dinner since the kids were in the mood for bite-size things. I don't know why we said yes to this because it's more work than it is just to make a pot of spaghetti."

"Pasta sounds pretty great right now. However, I'm good with appetizers. Let's go look at the list, since we promised our boys something fun."

We made our way to the kitchen, where Leif and Colin were both washing their hands, Colin on a step stool to reach, though he was getting tall enough now he would probably be able to reach soon. I wasn't sure when my boys had grown up, but here we were, making it work.

"Okay, let's start cooking," Sierra said after she washed her hands, looking down at her phone. "We each picked an appetizer, and now let's make something."

In the end, the four of us laughed in the kitchen, covered in flour and random vegetables. The scent of cooking food and spices filled my nostrils, my stomach groaned. I pulled out a beer, a root beer for the boys, and poured a glass of wine for Sierra, as we cooked and indulged in our favorite appetizers. My stomach rumbled for Dirty Martini Deviled Eggs and Zesty Meatballs.

We laughed, ate most of it while standing and waiting for the other parts to cook, since we were a little off on our timing, but it was family. It was hanging out and just being.

"I think I ate more than I should have, because they were so small and easy to pop into my mouth," Leif groaned, leaning against the couch.

I sighed. "I know what you mean. Just know that you won't be eating this well on campus. Eat what you want, but be healthy. And try not to only eat ramen."

Sierra leaned forward. "Or if you do eat ramen, add a vegetable or an egg. Protein."

Our son rolled his eyes. "Yes, because I'm going to hard-boil an egg in my dorm room on a hot plate because that sounds wonderful."

Colin started gagging and then giggled as Leif tickled him, and I shook my head, looking at my boys.

I couldn't help but think about the empty room upstairs, the one with the crib for the baby we had lost, and then for the children that we had almost had. We'd had contact with a birth mom and had begun the entire process of bringing home twins only a few short months ago. It had fallen through, the birth mom deciding to pick another family in the end. It had broken something in us, though we were healing, figuring out who we would be now.

I wasn't sure exactly when we would clear out that room, maybe make it another office or just a guest room. But it would have to be soon. The door was shut, I did my best not to think about it, and I knew Sierra did the same. Maybe after this weekend, with our first kid off to college and Colin growing by leaps and bounds, it'd be time to take that step.

We worked on the dishes, laughing together, and I'd pushed those thoughts from my mind when Sierra's phone rang. She answered it, a frown on her face before her eyes widened, and she sat on the stool as if she'd lost her balance.

I met Leif's gaze, worrying, as he took Colin out of the kitchen without another word. That kid understood me, and I was grateful for it.

I went to Sierra and took her hands, worried. "What's wrong?"

"Hold on, let me put you on speakerphone," she said, looking over her shoulder.

"Leif took him to the game room, music's on so he won't be able to hear us," I muttered.

"Mr. Montgomery, Mrs. Montgomery, I know this is a bad time and without notice, but I have some news."

"What news?"

"The other family that the birth mom had chosen has fallen through. Legal issues that I can't discuss or disclose, but the birth mom . . . she's in labor now. She's still going through with the adoption. If you're willing, it's going to be a lot of paperwork and no notice at all, and we're going to have a lot on our hands, but you need to come down to the hospital. She wants you there if you're still up for it. Yes or no. I will deal with all the paperwork and with everything that comes next, but you need to be there if you still want the twins."

I looked at Sierra, my mouth wide open.

"Just like that? After everything we went through?" I asked, my voice a growl. I couldn't feel anything. Emotions slamming into me I couldn't quite name or put in place. My hands went numb, and I just keep blinking. It didn't make any fucking sense.

Sierra cleared her throat. "Has she been in labor long? How is she?" Sierra asked softly, strong when I wasn't.

"She's just heading to the hospital now. It's her first child, but it is twins, as you know. You should get there if this is what you want, since that is what she wishes. If not, there are other avenues I can take, but the birth mom called me for you. So let me know."

Tears slid down Sierra's cheeks, and she let out a shaky breath. "Can I call you back in less than five minutes? I need to talk with my husband."

"Please," I growled.

"Of course. I know this is a huge decision after everything that you went through. I understand, and I'm here for you."

Sierra swallowed hard, hung up, and looked at me.

"Austin," she whispered.

"Are we fucking doing this? Do we have it in us?"

We weren't getting any younger, though I wasn't going to tell that to Sierra. But we had thought we'd be able to do this before, and we'd spent the past couple of months telling ourselves it would be okay that it wouldn't happen.

My wife paced the kitchen. "Leif. We're supposed to go tomorrow to search for colleges, Austin. Everything's changing. I don't want to do this to our boys."

"Jesus Christ, Sierra. I don't even understand. I was finally thinking about cleaning up the nursery, preparing ourselves to be grandparents at some point, and not parents raising babies."

"Do you think we can do this? I mean, would it be fair to the boys? There's no time to process. Nobody knows what we're doing. I can't understand how this is happening."

"We're going to have to talk about it more with them, but how? I wish we had more time to think about it."

"Don't worry about us," Leif said, Colin by his side.

I narrowed my eyes at him. "What happened to you being in the room with music?"

"We lied," Colin said, clapping his hands. "Don't worry about us. We've got it. We're ready to be big brothers. Right?" Colin asked, looking up at Leif with a grin.

Leif slid his hands into his hair and smiled, looking far older than I'd ever seen him. "Grandpa and Grandma can take me tomorrow. Or one of the three hundred aunts and uncles that I have. Talk about it with them. We're a big family. It's what we do. Or, heck, I can go any other time. That way, I'm here for my brothers and sisters, or whoever we get. We've got this."

Sierra moved forward. "It's a huge change, you guys. I know we discussed growing our family before, and we were all okay with it and ready. But it crushed us the first time, and I don't want to hurt you guys, ever." Sierra held Colin as I moved closer, wrapping my arms around Leif's shoulders.

We stood as a family of four, and I looked down at my boys and then at my wife. "We need to all be in on this. It's a huge change that we hadn't planned for. These are newborns. Twins."

"We've got this," Leif said. "I promise you. I can look at schools another weekend for all that matters. And I was already planning on staying in-state, so I can help you guys."

I shook my head vehemently. "No. You are not going to be raising these babies with us. But you're our kid too. We need to make sure this works."

We didn't have much longer to make the decision, so we talked about it, the pros and the cons, as quickly as we could, but as I looked at my wife and my kids, I knew what the answer would be, what it had to be.

I kissed my wife softly, then held my son and let out a shaky breath.

"Let's go meet the rest of our family," I whispered as Sierra wiped her tears, pulling out her phone. She called back the adoption agency while I called my brother, Wes. Wes would be able to organize the family phone tree and get the Montgomerys involved.

Once they were, we'd be able to handle anything.

At least that's what I told myself.

Sierra

In what felt like days, but was only a matter of hours, I stood wearing a hospital gown and shaking. Leif and Colin were in the waiting room with several of Austin's siblings. The other siblings were either watching the group of Montgomery babies or helping babyproof our house. We hadn't been prepared for this, and there were so many loose ends we were trusting in the hands of others. I was glad that we hadn't gotten rid of everything from when we had thought we would be bringing these babies home the first time. I had a million to-do lists in my head, but all I could focus on was holding my husband's hand as we waited in an empty room.

"I can't believe we're doing this," he said with a laugh, his blue eyes bright.

I looked up at him, went to my toes, and pressed my lips to his. "Is this a dream?"

"I don't think it is."

I loved my big husband, how growly he was, how sweet and sensitive he was. He was a protector, but caring in a way that most people didn't see.

He looked big and brash with his tattoos and long beard, and yet he'd put himself on the line for anybody.

He was the best father I knew, and now he would be a father to four kids—infants to nearly eighteen. It honestly didn't feel real.

"Are you ready?" he asked.

"Never, but with you, I think I can figure it out."

"Okay, Mom and Dad, are you ready to meet your babies?" a nurse asked from the doorway. Patricia, our contact with the adoption agency, stood beside us, tears in her eyes as she nodded at us.

We hadn't met with the birth mother, and wouldn't. It would be a closed adoption from here on out, and things would move forward. I couldn't think about the details, the process, or anything else. I just looked at the two bundles in the nurses' hands and held back tears.

One person held a blue bundle and slid it into my hands, while another slid a pink bundle into Austin's.

"Congratulations, Mom and Dad. Here are your babies."

I could barely see through the tears as I choked out a sob and looked at the tiny scrunched-up face in my hands. I shakily put one finger to his cheek and then looked down at the little girl in Austin's arms.

"I don't understand," I whispered, my body shaking.

Tears slid into Austin's beard as the nurses said things about passing their tests and everyone doing well.

"Welcome to the world, Gideon and Jamie," Austin breathed out, his voice rough. "Welcome to the Montgomerys."

And with that, I smiled wide, shaking my head. "Welcome to the world, Montgomerys," I whispered, and knowing that this wasn't going to be easy, that we were still only at the first step of the rest of our lives, and yet, we could do this. Somehow. We were going to do this.

Just one step at a time, with the man that I loved, the family that was all mine, and with these new lives that we knew we would cherish for all time.

Just a Bite

Zesty Meatballs

Jarcuterie Cups

Dirty Martini Deviled Eggs

Loaded Potato Dip

Blue Cheese Chicken Bites

Smoked Maple Bacon

ZESTY MEATBALLS

1 pound ground beef
½ cup panko bread crumbs
1 egg
¼ cup Parmesan cheese
1 can whole cranberry sauce
1 tablespoon soy sauce
⅓ cup apple cider vinegar
½ cup dark brown sugar

Preheat oven to 350 degrees. In a large bowl, combine ground beef, bread crumbs, egg, and Parmesan cheese. Roll into 1-inch balls. Place meatballs on a rimmed cookie sheet and bake for 30 minutes. Remove from oven. In a large pot on low heat or a crock pot on low, combine the whole cranberry sauce, soy sauce, apple cider vinegar, and brown sugar. Place the meatballs in the sauce and stir to cover. Cook on low, stirring occasionally, for 1 hour before serving.

QUICK TIP: *If you are in a hurry or simply don't want to make the meatballs, frozen Italian-style meatballs are just as delicious, and it can be our secret.* ☺ *Cook according to package directions before adding to zesty sauce.*

JARCUTERIE CUPS

Allow your inner artist to come out. Here is a fun palette of ingredients to paint with. You will need Mason jars to put your charcuterie in. Toothpicks are needed to display multiple items at a time.

Cheeses: sharp cheddar, mozzarella, pepper jack, and Parmesan
Cured meats: salami, pepperoni, and prosciutto
Fruit: blackberries, strawberries, raspberries, blueberries, and grapes
Bread: crackers, baguettes, or breadsticks
More fun: jams, jellies, honey, nuts, olives, pickles, and a Pepper Cheese Ball

Pepper Cheese Ball

1 (8 ounce) block cream cheese
2 ounces jalapeño pepper jelly
8-10 butter-flavored crackers, crushed (I use Ritz)

In a small bowl, combine cream cheese and pepper jelly. Place in the refrigerator for 30 minutes. Remove from refrigerator and form into 1-inch balls. Roll each ball in cracker crumbs. Refrigerate for at least 1 hour before serving.

DIRTY MARTINI DEVILED EGGS

6 hard-boiled eggs, cut in half
¼ cup mayonnaise
1 tablespoon olive juice (from green olive jar)
1 teaspoon dry vermouth
1 teaspoon dried parsley
½ teaspoon black pepper
6 green olives with pimentos, cut in half

In a small bowl, combine the egg yolks, mayonnaise, olive juice, dry vermouth, dried parsley, and black pepper. Fill each egg white with the egg yolk mixture and top with half of an olive slice.

LOADED POTATO DIP

16 ounces sour cream
1 (3 ounce) package bacon pieces
½ cup chopped green onion
1 cup shredded sharp cheddar cheese
1 teaspoon salt
1 teaspoon pepper
1 tablespoon mayonnaise
1 bag frozen waffle fries

In a large bowl, combine all ingredients except the waffle fries. Cover and place in the refrigerator for at least an hour to overnight before serving. Cook waffle fries according to package directions. Serve dip in a bowl with fries.

BLUE CHEESE CHICKEN BITES

4 boneless, skinless chicken breasts, cut into 48 pieces
16 slices bacon, cut into thirds
8 ounces blue cheese crumbles
½ cup wing sauce (I use Texas Pete)
¼ cup dark brown sugar

Preheat oven to 400 degrees. Place each piece of chicken in the center of a bacon slice. Top with about a teaspoon of blue cheese. Wrap bacon around chicken and cheese and secure with a toothpick. Place on parchment-lined, rimmed cookie sheet and bake for 15 minutes. While the chicken is baking, mix together the wing sauce and sugar in a small saucepan over low heat until combined and sugar has melted. Remove chicken from oven and brush sauce over each bite. Return to oven and bake for an additional 8-10 minutes or until bacon is crisp.

QUICK TIP: *If you aren't into spice, you can substitute your favorite BBQ sauce and still have a very delicious bite.*

SMOKED MAPLE BACON

12 slices thick-cut bacon
¼ cup maple syrup
½ cup dark brown sugar

Preheat smoker to 275 degrees. Place a cooking rack on top of a foil-lined rimmed baking sheet. Place bacon in a single layer on the rack. Brush the top side of each slice with maple syrup then sprinkle with brown sugar. Place baking sheet in the smoker and smoke for 20 minutes. Flip each slice of bacon, brush with maple syrup and sprinkle with brown sugar. Smoke for an additional 20 minutes. Remove from smoker and enjoy.

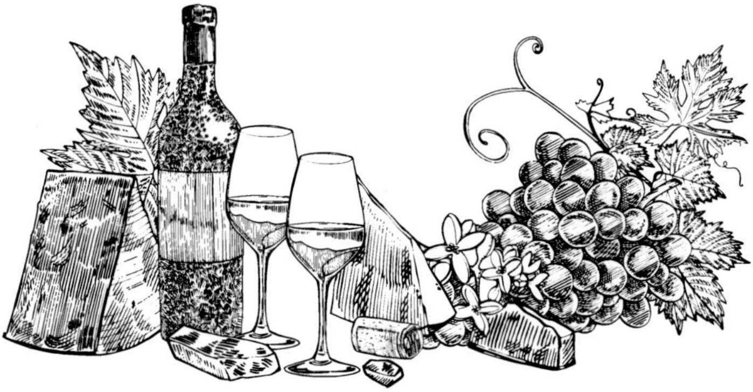

CHAPTER 2

Bring On the Temptations

Decker

When you have been married for over a decade, commercially made holidays such as Valentine's Day shouldn't be the be-all-end-all. However, I couldn't help but want to make my wife smile, and I had three kids who enjoyed the holiday, mainly because it came with candy.

Halloween was still their favorite celebration, even over Christmas. I felt kind of bad for my wife on that. She loved Christmas, it was her favorite holiday, so she went all out. Never to outdo anyone else, but to make sure the kids and I had the best time, even if sometimes cakes exploded in the oven.

The kids always had a decent time, and we did our best to make sure we spent half of our time giving to others, as the Montgomerys had always given to me as a child, versus focusing on what toys they could get.

Halloween, though, that was my holiday. I loved being able to dress up, scare the crap out of the kids, and make our house into the best haunted house there was in our family. The fact that I could even beat my brother-in-law, Wes, at it? Perfection. Because Wes and his wife Jillian loved Halloween too, but it was *my* holiday.

However, it was nowhere near that, and this week was all about Valentine's Day.

"I want to make sure that I get Kayleigh a good gift. You know? She's my girlfriend."

I met Miranda's gaze across the kitchen island as she pressed her lips together, trying not to smile.

Micah was eleven now, which still shocked me to this day that I had an eleven-year-old son, and he had a girlfriend.

Not an actual girlfriend where they went on dates, but one where they sometimes sat with each other at lunch and nodded at each other on the playground.

It was a Big Deal, complete with capital letters, for my kid.

Evelyn, our nine-year-old, was thinking about getting a boyfriend, but she couldn't choose between two. When she had said that she wanted to be like her aunt Maya who had two husbands, she figured why not.

I was going to leave that conversation to her aunt and mother because I was not getting into the topic of polyamorous relationships and monogamy with my nine-year-old.

I held back a groan, wondering why the hell I had married into a family with so many siblings. There were enough Montgomerys that we stretched across the rainbow, and I had around thirty nieces and nephews at this point, with more coming in from around the state with Miranda's cousins.

The upcoming family reunion might actually kill me, as we had to rent out a resort up in Boulder, near where one of Miranda's cousins had a cabin of his own. We didn't fit in any of the multiple homes that any of us owned. Felt a little ridiculous. Then I remembered that I had been part of this family long before I had fallen for my best friend.

Pia, our youngest at six, came up to the island, climbed her way on top of the stool, and set her chin on her hands, grinning up at me.

I was a little afraid of that look. Micah and I were far outnumbered in this family, and it was worrying.

"Hi."

I held back laughter. "Hi, Pia. What can I do for you?"

"I don't want a boyfriend or a girlfriend. But can I have chocolate to give to myself? You always said you have to love yourself. And since I love myself the mostest, I should get chocolate."

I couldn't hold it back any longer. Instead, I threw my head back and laughed as Miranda put her head in her hands, giggling with me.

"Well, I want to give myself chocolate too," Evelyn said, bouncing on her stool. "This way, I choose myself over the boys. That's perfect. I don't need a boyfriend."

I grinned, thinking that was a good idea. Pia had solved all my problems. "You know what, maybe you should give chocolate to each other."

Miranda just rolled her eyes. "I guess that works. Would you use your allowances for it? Or do you want to use the Mommy and Daddy Fund?"

The Mommy and Daddy Fund was for small gifts and luxuries that had nothing to do with an allowance, but just because. Miranda had come up with the idea, and I hadn't always been okay with it, but then I realized why she was doing it.

Because I had grown up with nothing.

My dad had been a world-class abusive jerk who had hurt me and my mother beyond anything I ever wanted to dwell on. And my mom had chosen him over me countless times. I hadn't gotten the candy and cupcakes and random temptations that were far too indulgent for most kids. I hadn't gotten anything. All I had had was a fist to the face and losing something precious.

I would never give that to my kids. So we allowed our kids to spoil themselves and let us cherish them with a few things. They had to work for most fun things, but they never had to work for our love, the roof over their head, or their full bellies. They always had that.

Miranda moved over to me and wrapped her arms around my waist. I looked down at her and grinned before I pressed my lips to hers.

All three kids cheered, none of them gagging or making squealing noises, and I counted that as a win.

Miranda winked as she leaned back. "Okay, so when you guys are at school, and I am at school with you, since my days are just as fun as yours in the classroom, your daddy gets to go shopping."

I cringed but nodded. I worked for Montgomery Inc. and worked my ass off with Miranda's family. I had been brought in as a full partner a couple of years ago, rather than working directly for Wes, who was the lead contractor. I hadn't needed that, hadn't even wanted it, but they had. Because Miranda was a Montgomery by blood, I legally changed my name to Montgomery when we got married. I hadn't needed my former last name. Kendrick hadn't meant anything to me. But Montgomery did. Because it was the Montgomerys that had brought me in, long before I had allowed myself to fall for Miranda, the Montgomerys had housed me, clothed me, and fed me. I had practically lived at their place for much of high school, and then sometimes afterward.

That's why falling for Miranda had been the one thing I hadn't wanted to do until it had been inevitable.

Each of the Montgomery siblings had a small portion of Montgomery Inc. in their name. Most had sold it back to the siblings who worked at the company, especially those who owned the other Montgomery Ink, the tattoo shop.

Miranda had sold hers when she had turned eighteen and had used it to pay for school. But we bought back into the company, this time with the family wanting to make sure they knew I was a Montgomery through and through.

All it meant was that I was part of the family, even though I had already known that, and nothing had changed, other than the fact that I was getting older and had my own staff now. I was still decently in shape, but there was only so much heavy lifting I could do, especially when I have to come home and play ball with the kids or have a little too much fun with my wife once the sun set.

Speaking of, I swallowed hard, trying to ignore the thoughts of what Miranda and I would be doing later on that weekend. We had finally hired a babysitter.

It would be just us, a decadent dinner made for the two of us, just at home. We weren't going to deal with the crowds outside, we were going to get decently dolled up, in Miranda's words, and then I was going to strip that dress off her, bend her over the table, and fuck her hard just like we used to do day-in and day-out when we'd first gotten married.

Our sex life was still good, beyond good. It was just a little harder to tiptoe into the bedroom, lock the door so that there weren't any unfortunate incidents, and keep quiet.

And keeping Miranda quiet with the two of us? It wasn't easy.

Miranda seemed to know where my mind went, and she raised a brow, a blush staining her cheeks. She was so beautiful. It was hard even to breathe sometimes. However, I had to focus on what was in front of me, and it was not my wife.

"Just make me a list," I said after a moment, aware that everyone was staring at me for an answer. "A detailed list. Preferably with photos. That way, I know what I'm getting. I'm decently good at guessing things, but if you want something special for your girlfriend, you've got to let me know."

Micah rolled his eyes. "You don't have to sneer when you say girlfriend."

"I do, mostly because it's fun to mess with you. However, make me a list and a budget, and I'll get it done."

"Thank you, babe," Miranda replied as she kissed me softly, and the kids cheered again.

I rolled my eyes and then pushed them out of the kitchen so they could work on their homework with Miranda while I began dinner, the Cajun Chicken Pasta Alfredo making my mouth water.

It was probably a little too self-indulgent for a Sunday evening meal, but why not? Valentine's Day was coming up soon, and we were going to get filled with chocolate and whatever I made Miranda later.

By the time the next Friday rolled around and the kids had their Valentine's Day parties, and after a few setbacks at work, the project taking up more time than it should have, I was exhausted. It wasn't anything to do with the Montgomerys. We knew what the fuck we were doing, but no, the clients who were having us rehab one of their old mansions kept changing things, and everything had to be approved by the historical society, and then and there, I knew I would never work with that company again.

Graham Gallagher came to my side as I was finishing up, shaking his head.

"Next time we say no," Graham said, and I nodded, rubbing the back of my neck.

"Never again."

Graham and his brothers owned another restoration company, with the Gallaghers being at the forefront of this project with us. They needed the manpower of the Montgomerys, but we needed their expertise, so we were working together. It helped that Graham's brother Jake was one of Maya's husbands, so we were all family anyway.

We had decided to not combine the companies under one umbrella because family was important, as was the separation of our expertise. Still, we tended to work on at least one project a year together, the same with the Montgomery builders up in Fort Collins.

"You heading home?" I asked Graham, and he nodded.

"Valentine's Day with the kids at school means they're all hyped up on sugar, and then I get to spend time with my wife."

I laughed. "My kids are with the babysitter tonight."

"Really? Not at your house?" Graham asked, and I shook my head.

"No, Stacey has a whole setup, and we've done it before. She used to be a full-time nanny. She's retired, but she still has the setup in her house. Works out for us because it's like a hotel for the kids, and they get a vacation, and I get to spend the night alone with my wife."

I raised my brows as Graham laughed. "Oh yes, alone time with the wife. I can remember that with Blake."

"She working all day?" Blake was the piercer and tattoo artist at Montgomery Ink with some of my in-laws.

"Yes, and working pretty late tonight with a customer that needed next week off because of travel."

I frowned. "Really?"

"She's heading to stay with her mom to help with hospice care, so Blake said she would work on the tattoo so her mom can see it before everything turns." Graham ran his hand over his face, looking exhausted.

I shook my head, reached out, and squeezed the man's shoulder. "I'm sorry about that. But Blake's doing a good thing."

"Yeah, my wife's pretty fantastic. It would be nice if I got to see her sometime."

I laughed at that, knowing that Blake and Graham spent every waking moment they could together, and their marriage was solid as hell. It was just a long day, and I knew he wanted to be home with his wife as much as I did.

"Well, I need to go make sure the kids get to Stacey's safe, and then start dinner."

"You doing your indulgence fest?"

"All the temptations," I said with a laugh, knowing the others were making fun of my cooking skills, but they had gotten better over the years. I no longer just grilled meat with a baked potato on the side. I cooked well, and the cooking classes I took with Miranda meant a lot of trial and error.

But a lot of kissing to make up for it in the end.

I made it home and walked in to the kids talking a mile a minute and Miranda giving me a cringing smile.

"Stacey has a cold, came out of nowhere, so the kids are going to be helping us with dinner tonight." She clapped her hands, and all thoughts of sexy times and me finally tying my woman up and fucking her hard from behind while she begged for an orgasm fled.

There would be no hot sex tonight, no chocolate sauce across her chest, no her begging me as I slowly teased her entrance.

No, tonight would be family.

I looked at my kids, then at my wife, and shrugged. "Okay, I see my four Valentines here. Let's get started."

"Yay!" All the kids yelled, thoughts of missing out long forgotten.

By the time we made our dishes, the addition of Whiskey Honey Ribs filling to the point that we would have leftovers for a week, the kids were stuffed. Later, their food comas had finally taken over the chocolate sugar intakes, and we watched a movie as a family, the three kids separating Miranda and me. I slid my hand over the back of the couch, tangling my fingers with hers, and I just smiled at her. She beamed up at me, my best friend's little sister, my wife, and I knew that this was fine. It wasn't exactly what we had planned, but it was still pretty damn perfect.

We tucked the kids into bed, and then I rolled my shoulders back, figuring after this long of a day, we should head to bed and plan for a weekend out later. Between our family and Stacey, when she was better, I'd find a night for my wife.

"Knock knock," Miranda whispered, and I looked up to see her with her back to the door, a robe on, and a piece of Gooey Butter Cake that I had made the night before in her hand.

"I thought we were full?"

"Oh, I'm not full yet," she whispered as she locked the door behind her, winked, and set the cake on the table in front of me.

"What are you doing?"

"I think I can be quiet, can you?"

And then she undid the robe, and my mouth watered.

She wore a tiny strip of lace between her legs, her generous curves calling my name. She had on a small bustier that plumped up her breasts but left her nipples bare, the hard little points begging for my mouth.

"When did you have time to get that on?"

"I was quick, so you're going to have to untie it for me slowly, so we don't rip it, then I'm going to need you to remind me how much fun we can have if we're quiet. Because it's been a very long time, husband, and I miss you."

I groaned, kissed her hard, and smiled.

"What about the cake?"

"I'm pretty sure we can eat that too. But first, you have another dessert to eat." Then she slid my hand between her legs, and I found her wet, and both of us sighed.

Yes, this was my Valentine, and I was one lucky man.

Miranda

The following morning, I groaned as the light bit into my eyes, and I looked over at my husband and smiled, sated and happy. I got up, stretched, and winced. I needed to do more yoga or something if we were going to have those late nights.

I looked at the clock and blinked. How the heck was it 8 a.m.?

I shook my head, crawled out of bed, and tried to leave Decker asleep before I slid on sweat shorts and a T-shirt and made my way out. If the kids were already awake, they had been quiet, but a little too quiet. I tiptoed into the kitchen and smiled to see all three of my babies eating cereal in the breakfast nook, a cartoon on the tablet in front of them as they shared. They all snuggled close before Micah smiled up at me.

"Happy day after Valentine's Day, Mom."

"Happy day after Valentine's Day, babies."

I started the pot of coffee then made my way to the bench nook. I leaned forward, kissed the tops of their heads, and then poured myself a bowl of cereal. My stomach was a little full after our way too yummy food the night before, but that was fine with me.

I slid into the nook with Pia, let her rest her head on my shoulder as she watched the show and continued to eat, and I looked at my kids and grinned. When Decker came in a few minutes later, a T-shirt and sweats on, he poured us two cups of coffee and sat down on the other side next to Evelyn. I looked across the bench seats at my husband and smiled.

And as we talked about how our day would go, what chores we needed to do, and the errands that we needed to run, I knew that somehow I had lucked into the best decisions in the world. I hadn't planned on Decker, although he had always been the man of my dreams.

Now he was the man of my reality, and everything I needed.

Bring on the Temptations

Cajun Chicken Pasta Alfredo

Whiskey Honey Ribs

Orange Chicken

French Dip Au Jus

Bold Burger

CAJUN CHICKEN PASTA ALFREDO

Cajun Seasoning

1 teaspoon salt
1 teaspoon pepper
1 teaspoon cayenne pepper
1 teaspoon onion powder
1 teaspoon garlic powder
1 teaspoon paprika

1 (8 ounce) package fettuccine pasta
4 boneless, skinless chicken breasts
4 tablespoons butter
8 ounces cream cheese
2 cups heavy cream
1 cup grated Parmesan cheese

In large bowl, combine salt, pepper, cayenne, onion powder, garlic powder, and paprika to make the Cajun seasoning. Prepare noodles according to package directions. Cut each chicken breast into approximately 12 bite-size pieces and toss in Cajun seasoning. In a large skillet over medium heat, sauté seasoned chicken in butter for 8-10 minutes, making sure to brown all sides. Reduce heat to low and stir in cream cheese and heavy cream. Stir constantly until well combined and smooth. Stir in Parmesan cheese and allow to simmer for 8-10 minutes. Fold in pasta and serve.

QUICK TIP: I use freshly grated Parmesan cheese for a smoother finish. The "shaky shake" kind does NOT work. Fresh is best for this recipe. I literally grate it directly into the skillet.

WHISKEY HONEY RIBS

1-2 pounds baby back ribs
Cajun seasoning (page 26)
1 cup mesquite BBQ sauce (I use Stubb's)
½ cup honey
1 shot bourbon (I use Makers Mark)

Using a sharp knife, remove silver skin from ribs along the rack. Rinse ribs and thoroughly pat dry. Combine the ingredients for the Cajun seasoning and cover the ribs entirely, being liberal with coverage. Allow to set for 10-15 minutes at room temperature. Heat one side of grill to medium-high heat. Place ribs on opposite side so that the ribs cook over indirect heat. Combine the BBQ sauce, honey and bourbon in a small bowl. Baste ribs every 10 minutes with the whiskey honey sauce for a total cooking time of 45-55 minutes. Remove ribs from heat and double wrap in aluminum foil. Return to grill on low heat and cook for an additional 20-25 minutes. Remove from grill and allow to rest for 10 minutes before slicing.

ORANGE CHICKEN

1 cup orange juice

½ cup sugar

2 tablespoons white vinegar

2 tablespoons soy sauce

¼ teaspoon ginger

¼ teaspoon garlic powder

1/3 cup cornstarch plus 1 tablespoon

1/3 cup all-purpose flour

3 eggs

4 boneless, skinless chicken breasts cut into 1-inch pieces

3-4 cups oil for frying

In a large pot over low heat, stir together orange juice, sugar, vinegar, soy sauce, ginger, and garlic powder for 3-5 minutes or until sugar is dissolved. In a small bowl, whisk together one tablespoon cornstarch with 2 tablespoons COLD water. Pour into orange sauce and whisk for 3-5 minutes to allow sauce to thicken. Remove from heat and set aside. To make chicken, add the flour and remaining cornstarch to a large plate and stir to combine. In a large bowl, whisk eggs and 2 tablespoons of water. Dip each piece of chicken into egg mixture and then flour mixture, making sure to coat, but shaking off excess. Heat oil in a Dutch oven or iron skillet to 350 degrees. Add 6-8 pieces of chicken to the oil and fry for 3-4 minutes until golden brown. Place on a paper towel-lined cookie sheet. Repeat with remaining chicken. Toss chicken in orange sauce and serve immediately.

FRENCH DIP AU JUS

1 (16 ounce) sirloin steak
1 teaspoon salt
1 teaspoon pepper
3 sweet onions, thinly sliced
1 tablespoon minced garlic
32 ounces beef broth
¼ cup mayonnaise
4 hoagie rolls
8 slices provolone cheese

Preheat oven to 350 degrees. Season steak with salt and pepper and place in a 9 x 13-inch baking dish. Cover with onions and garlic and pour beef broth into the dish. Cover with foil and bake for 2 hours. Remove from oven and shred the steak using 2 forks. Spread mayonnaise over both sides of the hoagie rolls and place on a cookie sheet. Place in the already heated oven for 10 minutes or until bread is lightly toasted. Remove from oven and place about ½ cup to 1 cup of shredded beef and onions on each roll. Top with 2 slices of provolone cheese and bake for an additional 5 minutes or until the cheese is melted. Serve with Au Jus. The Au Jus is the sauce the steak was cooked in. Simply ladle the sauce into a small bowl for serving.

BOLD BURGER

1 pound ground beef
½ cup grated Parmesan cheese
Salt and pepper to taste
8 slices 5-cheese garlic toast (I use Pepperidge Farm)
1 (8 ounce) jar pizza sauce
4 slices fresh mozzarella cheese

In a large bowl, combine ground beef, grated Parmesan and salt and pepper to taste. Form into 4-inch patties. Preheat grill to medium and cook burgers for 10-12 minutes, turning halfway through, or until 160 degrees for medium (170 degrees for well done). While the burgers are grilling, bake the garlic toast according to package directions. To build your burger, place 4 slices of toast cheese side up. Spread evenly with pizza sauce, then top with burger and mozzarella cheese. Top with remaining 4 slices of garlic toast, placing the cheese side down to make 4 delicious burgers.

CHAPTER 3

Spice it Up!

Luc

There were times when I knew exactly what to say. When I was ready to face the oncoming questions of being a father of four and to settle any problem that came my way. My kids were the center of my world, just like my wife.

Yet something was bothering my oldest daughter, and I could not figure out what it was.

And neither could Meghan, with the way that she kept looking at me as if I had all the answers. The problem was, I used to. I used to have those answers. At least it felt like it. But then again, so had Meghan. And now here we were, staring at each other as our teenage daughter grumbled something to herself, looking completely lost and angry at the world, and I didn't know how to fix it.

"Sasha? Is there something that you want to tell us?" Meghan asked as she reached out and gripped my hand. I looked down at her slender wrist and wanted to pull it to my lips for a kiss. Only it wasn't the right time, and I was afraid if we didn't take a break from the necessities that were our life, we might not ever find that time again.

"Nothing's wrong." The clipped sound of my daughter's voice split the air, and I let out a breath.

"Sasha. There's got to be something wrong if you're not talking to us."

"Why do I have to tell you everything? I'm eighteen. I'm not a little girl anymore. I'm having a bad day. Maybe it's just my period."

"You talking about menstruation isn't going to push me away from this conversation. It's a new age. I'm not going to wince."

"Ugh! Why can't you be like any normal guy and just walk away as soon as I talk about anything girl problem related?"

"Because I have two daughters, a wife, and fifty thousand Montgomery cousins. Not to mention your aunts. You're not going to push me away by saying those things. Talk to me."

My daughter, who didn't look a thing like me since we didn't share a single biological gene, blinked up at me before she burst into tears. I cursed under my breath as my wife and I moved forward. We hugged Sasha close, helpless.

"Baby, talk to us. What's wrong?"

"I'm fine," Sasha bit out as she leaned into us.

"You just burst out crying, and you're angry for seemingly no reason. There's got to be a reason."

"Fine. Marcus dumped me."

I blinked and looked back at her. "I thought you and Marcus were just friends?"

She rolled her eyes, let out a huff. "Dad."

"Don't Dad me. When did you become more than friends? How could he have broken up with you when you weren't dating?"

"Luc, darling, one thing at a time."

"I think this is the same thing."

"Oh, so you're fine with talking about menstruation, but suddenly I talk about boyfriends, and you freak out like a dad from the '50s?"

I pinched the bridge of my nose and waved Cliff off.

Cliff was sixteen and nearly as tall as I was, and his eyes were wide. He put his hands on both Emma's and Benjamin's shoulders.

As Benjamin was eight, and Emma was ten, they had an inkling of what we were talking about, so therefore my eldest son seemed to read my mind. He pulled the kids away, and out to the backyard where hopefully he would watch them for a minute while I figured out what the hell was going on with my oldest daughter.

Meghan and I had been married for over a decade now. We had been through hell and back multiple times, and I still felt like I was sometimes scrambling when it came to my kids.

"Talk to us," Meghan whispered.

"Fine. Marcus and I were just friends. And then he asked me out. On a date. I haven't gone out with him, but before we could even plan the first one and I could tell you guys about it because I don't like to keep secrets from you, he broke up with me."

My mind tried to catch up with everything that she was saying, and I nodded along.

"I'm sorry." I wasn't sure what else to say.

"Did he tell you why? Why would he act like that? It just seems so different from the Marcus that we know."

Sasha shrugged and then pulled her long dark hair, which was so much like her mother's, away from her face. "Marcus found out about Dad."

I frowned, wondering what the hell he could find out about, and then it hit me.

Not me, the other one.

That one.

The last time I had seen the other man had been in a courthouse, going through a parole hearing, and before that, it had been his actual court case, and before that, it had been when he had shot me.

My shoulder ached thinking about it, and I rolled it back and froze as soon as I did. Both Meghan's and Sasha's faces winced at the action, and I cursed.

"Sorry. It doesn't hurt. Just muscle memory."

"That's a problem, isn't it? So many memories. Marcus found out dear old biological Dad is in jail for attempted murder and a few other white-collar crimes. I know we moved neighborhoods, we moved school districts, so it wasn't as big of a deal growing up because you guys are amazing, but apparently, now it's all over social media."

Meghan began to pace, her arms folded over her chest. "It's such old news. They know you. It shouldn't be an issue. I'm so sorry, baby." She held out her hands and kissed Sasha on the top of her head. Sasha was slight, a little pixie, compared to Meghan's slightly above average height.

Sasha was still my baby girl, just like Emma was.

And I wanted to rip the arms off this bastard teenage boy who had dared hurt my baby.

"I see the growl you're making, and you don't need to. I'm not upset that Marcus broke up with me."

I rubbed my temple. "Can you just explain that to me? Because now I'm confused."

"Same here," Meghan added.

"I'm not upset that Marcus broke up with me because it wasn't going to work out anyway. Not when he was so flip-floppy when it comes to emotions." She met my gaze. "I'm very spoiled with you and my uncles, and even my brother," she said with a sneer. "I like guys who tell me what they're feeling, so I don't have to read their minds. You think it's a woman's problem when they have to read their minds, but it's not. It's a person problem. Anyway, I was happy, it was nice. I was going on a date. And then he brought up all this crap about my dad."

Meghan let out a breath. "I'm so sorry. I wish there were something I could do."

"I know he's in jail for a long time, and there's another parole hearing coming up, but I don't know. It just feels weird. That part of my life feels like a memory, and yet, some part of me, I don't know. I don't want to see him," she added, her hands up.

Meghan's shoulders dropped as if relief had hit her like a freight train. I reached out and hugged my wife close to me, wrapping my arm around her shoulders. She leaned into me, and Sasha smiled softly.

"See? The two of you didn't even speak. You just held on to each other and relaxed as if you're two parts of a whole. I want that, eventually, when I'm ready. First, I need to become a high-powered lawyer and a partner at a firm. And after that, then I can find love."

I met Meghan's gaze, my lips twitching before we looked back at our daughter.

"You know you can't plan to fall in love, right?" Meghan asked.

"No, but I figured I could at least try to plan it a bit. I mean, things work out when they need to, I guess, but it's not like your generation. I can make things work my way."

Every time my daughter said something like that, I felt like I was getting a little older, a little closer to death. I wasn't in my twenties anymore, and hell, I wasn't even in my thirties anymore, and Sasha was a pro about reminding me that I was an old man, part of a generation that didn't understand the new kids.

And the times that she reminded me, I made sure to send my mother flowers, just to say I was sorry for being the idiot that I had been when I was my daughter's age.

"Thank you for reminding me that I'm old," Meghan added with a grin. "Do you need to go see Dr. Rogers?"

Dr. Rogers was our psychiatrist, a newer one who had fit in with our family once we had grown away from the original family and trauma specialist. Dr. Rogers had helped us figure out exactly where we needed to be in terms of this new life of ours. One where we didn't blame ourselves for everything that had happened, but we didn't tend to go as much as we used to.

"Maybe. I don't know. It's just frustrating, Daddy," she said, and my heart twisted. She didn't call me Daddy often, my little girl was all grown up. "I know you're my dad. I know that we went through all the adoption paperwork and that asshole, sorry for my language, cut all ties from us. I know that he has nothing to do with me. I just hate the fact that he's there. That people can look it up and bring it up. I hate that we go out as a family, and people don't realize that Emma and Benjamin are my brother and sister because we don't look alike. I hate that they don't realize that you're my dad because we have no looks in common. I hate it all. And I don't know. I'm just grumbling."

I held out my arms again, and she sank into me before I looked at my wife.

Meghan kissed Sasha's forehead. "We don't have answers, Sasha. But we're here for you. Always."

"I wish we had answers," I put in. "But your mom's right, we're here for you. Always. Screw what people think about our family, what they look up on the internet. We're us. You are a Montgomery-Dodd. A very long name that's going to look wonderful on letterhead when you're that high-powered lawyer."

Sasha leaned back and grinned at me. "I like the sound of that. Sasha Montgomery-Dodd, Attorney at Law. It'll be nice to have more lawyers in the family, don't you think?"

Meghan rubbed her temples. "We tried so hard to make sure you were a blue-collar worker, and now you're going off to go take over the world. I see how it is." Meghan leaned forward, cupped our daughter's cheeks. "I love you, baby. I hate that the world thinks that they can have any opinion when it comes to us. But screw that. We are family, and that's all that matters. Now, why don't we make a batch of Peach Pepper Jelly Grilled Chicken? It's spicy, yummy, and one of your favorites."

Sasha's eyes brightened. "You know what? I'm not a little kid. You can't just feed me some of my favorite foods to make all the pain go away."

I swallowed hard. "But we could try. Why not? Food makes me happy. And we'll talk withCed Dr. Rogers if you'd like. I can go beat up that little boy of yours if you'd like as well. I mean, he is eighteen, he's an adult, he deserves it."

Sasha winced. "Please don't. Because then that's just a whole other thing that they can look up on the internet."

"I'll never regret marrying the man who gave you your side of your DNA," Meghan added after a minute, surprising me. Sasha's eyes widened. I had a feeling her thoughts were just as jumbled as mine.

"Seriously. Because it brought me you and Cliff. I try not to think about him because he's not important. All he did was bring two of my favorite parts of my life into this world. Now it's the six of us—the six of us against the world. There's no one like us. Our extended family may be huge, and we have hundreds of people to lean on if we need to, but in the end, it's this core. This is who we are. Screw what anyone else thinks, what they possibly could imagine they can do to split us apart. They can't hurt us because we are the ones that make our path and our future. We, as a team, you and me and Cliff, decided who we were going to be, and we let Luc into our lives."

"I'll be forever blessed that you did," I whispered.

My wife looked up at me and grinned. "Exactly. It's the six of us. Now, I know I have all the ingredients for this recipe, let's go get your brothers and sister, and we're going to cook, eat, and watch a movie."

"It's a school night," Sasha added. "We can't stay up too late."

"I'm calling you all out for tomorrow," Meghan added with a shrug, and I blinked.

"Excuse me, darling?"

"What? We're calling out to work too. We own the business. We'll do what we want. I'm sure that our families will understand, after all, we work far too many hours even though we keep telling ourselves we won't. We are taking a rest day, a mental health day. Or whatever the hell you want to call it. But we will eat some food, maybe even bake a cake if I still feel like it, and then we are going to sit down, watch as many movies as we want, and do nothing. Because why not?"

Sasha laughed. "Setting a great example for the little ones."

"I think we'll manage." Meghan kissed our daughter's forehead, and I looked up to see Cliff running into the house after Emma and Benjamin.

"Did I hear we're not going to school tomorrow?" Cliff asked, sauntering in. "Hell yeah."

"Language," Meghan snapped, and Cliff winced before he pulled a dollar out of his pocket and put it in the swear jar.

Emma and Benjamin danced around us, and we all walked into the kitchen.

Out of the corner of my eye, I saw Sasha pull out a dollar to put into the swear jar, and I knew we had raised a pretty damn good child. We hadn't even called her out on her swearing earlier, but she was doing the right thing.

I hadn't meant to fall in love with my best friend twice. And yet here I was, father of four and husband to the sexiest, most brilliant woman that I knew.

And every time I woke up, even as the aches and pains from aging, as my children routinely reminded me, intensified, I was still here.

I looked around at my family and grinned. And I wasn't going anywhere.

Meghan

Stuffed full of spicy food and cake, I lay on top of Luc on the couch, Benjamin sprawled on top of me as he drooled in his sleep. Emma was somehow wrapped around Luc and bumping into my head with each snore.

Cliff and Sasha were on the floor, Sasha's back to the couch, as Cliff slept on her shoulder.

We were a tangle of limbs, and I knew Luc and I would be hurting the next morning, since we were way too old to be sleeping on the couch at these angles, but I didn't care.

I hated my first husband. He was nothing but pain, heartache, and memories that I had done my best to ignore. I couldn't forget them, that hadn't been healthy for me, but I could move past them. And I had.

But I will never forgive him for hurting my kids. They weren't his. The fact that Sasha had called him Dad today had just been a slip of the tongue. She rarely called him anything other than that asshole. And he was. His parole hearing was coming up in the next six months, and I would testify, and so would Luc, and so would countless others.

The man I had married, the man who had tried to kill Luc, and the man who had ruined everything, would get out eventually. His sentence wasn't a lifetime term, though it wasn't the attempted murder and abuse and assault that had gotten him in for so many years. No, it was the white-collar crimes of embezzling and fraud that had sent him to jail for so long. I tried not to think about the system that allowed that to happen but focus on the family that I had.

I hadn't expected them, and I would never, ever, take them for granted.

We were in the middle of our future, the middle of the life that I hadn't expected to have.

And as I looked at my sleeping husband, my crashed kids, I just grinned, knowing that the neck pain and back pain I would have tomorrow from waking up like this would be worth it.

It always was.

Spice It Up!

Buffalo Chicken Stuffed Bread

Peach Pepper Jelly Grilled Chicken

Spicy Corn Chowder

Beef Curry Stir Fry

Memphis Chicken

BUFFALO CHICKEN STUFFED BREAD

1 French loaf
1 (8 ounce) block cream cheese
4 cups cooked chicken, shredded
2 cups shredded cheddar cheese
½ cup hot sauce
¼ cup chopped green onion
1 tablespoon ranch seasoning
2 tablespoons melted butter

Preheat oven to 425 degrees. Using a serrated knife, cut a slice of bread from one end of the loaf. Using your hands, hollow out the loaf. In a medium bowl, combine cream cheese, chicken, cheddar cheese, hot sauce, green onion, and ranch seasoning. Spoon chicken mixture into hollowed out bread and place slice back onto the end of the loaf. Brush the loaf with melted butter and wrap in foil. Bake covered for 20 minutes, then uncovered for 5 additional minutes.

PEACH PEPPER JELLY GRILLED CHICKEN

2 cups diced peaches, fresh or canned

3 tablespoons oil

2 tablespoons Dijon mustard

3 tablespoons soy sauce

1 (4 ounce) jar jalapeño pepper jelly

6-8 boneless, skinless chicken breasts

Salt and pepper to taste

In a large bowl, combine peaches, oil, Dijon mustard, soy sauce and pepper jelly. Cover and refrigerate for 30 minutes. Reserve ½ cup of glaze for later. Preheat grill to 350 degrees. Season chicken breasts with salt and pepper and place on the grill. Cook for 8-10 minutes on each side. Next, brush one side with the glaze and cook for 2-3 minutes. Turn the chicken and brush with the glaze to grill for an additional 2-3 minutes. Remove from grill and serve with reserved glaze.

SPICY CORN CHOWDER

4 tablespoons butter

1 sweet onion, chopped

1 jalapeño, diced

1 teaspoon minced garlic

¼ cup all-purpose flour

4 cups chicken broth

1 cup frozen hash brown potatoes

1 cup heavy cream

1 (15 ounce) can corn

½ teaspoon cayenne pepper

In a large stockpot over medium heat, melt butter and sauté onion for about 5 minutes. Add in jalapeño and garlic and sauté for 2 minutes. Stir in flour until a roux forms (about 1 minute). Add in the chicken broth and potatoes and stir until blended. Simmer on low for 10 minutes. Add in heavy cream, corn, and cayenne pepper and simmer for an additional 15-20 minutes.

BEEF CURRY STIR FRY

1 (16 ounce) sirloin steak, cut into ¼-inch strips

3 tablespoons soy sauce

1 tablespoon minced garlic

1 teaspoon ground ginger

¼ cup oil

1 large onion, thinly sliced

1 green bell pepper, thinly sliced

1 red bell pepper, thinly sliced

4 teaspoons cornstarch

2 teaspoons curry powder

Cooked white rice

In a large bowl, add steak, soy sauce, garlic, ginger and 2 tablespoons oil, then toss to coat. Cover and refrigerate for 30 minutes. In a large skillet or wok over medium high heat, add remaining oil and beef with marinade. Stir fry for 3-4 minutes, then remove beef and set aside. In the same skillet, stir fry the onion and bell peppers for 3-4 minutes, then return the beef to the skillet. In a small bowl, combine the cornstarch, curry powder and 1 cup COLD water, then pour into the skillet. Bring skillet to a boil for 1 minute, stirring constantly. Serve over rice.

MEMPHIS CHICKEN

1 tablespoon chili powder plus 1 teaspoon
1 teaspoon black pepper plus 1 teaspoon
1 teaspoon onion powder plus 1 teaspoon
1 teaspoon garlic powder plus 1 teaspoon
1 teaspoon salt plus 1 teaspoon
4 chicken leg quarters

¼ cup dark brown sugar
1 cup ketchup
¼ cup mustard
3 tablespoons apple cider vinegar
1 tablespoon Worcestershire sauce

Using a smoker, heat to 300 degrees. In a small bowl, combine 1 teaspoon each of chili powder, pepper, onion powder, garlic powder, and salt. Rub over chicken and place on smoker. Smoke, turning every 20 minutes, for 1 hour. Then baste with sauce, smoke for 10 minutes, turn chicken, baste with sauce and smoke for an additional 10 minutes. To make sauce, combine remaining ingredients in a small pot over low heat and simmer for 10 minutes.

CHAPTER 4

All About the Veggies

Griffin

That's it. I had died and gone to a special heaven. One just for me, where the woman in front of me danced in just my button-up shirt. And nothing else. I groaned and leaned against the doorway as Autumn danced to music in her head, shaking those hips as if she were leading me into temptation, and I was following right in.

Every time she lifted one hip, the bottom of her ass cheek showed beneath the shirt, and I groaned, adjusting myself in my sweats.

I cleared my throat, and Autumn whirled, knife in hand, eyes wide. "What the hell were you doing?" she screamed.

I had both hands up, my own eyes wide. "I'm just admiring the dancing. And your ass. I didn't want to scare you. Apparently, I failed."

Autumn set the knife down, the platter of veggies forgotten. She put her hand over her chest and let out a breath. "You scared me. I thought you were going to kill me."

I cursed under my breath, then moved forward to cup her face. I kissed her softly. She tasted of chicory coffee and the beignets we had had earlier. We were renting a house in New Orleans and had come back after our breakfast at a popular beignet destination before we'd enjoyed breakfast in bed. There was powdered sugar everywhere, and not even one shower had helped clean it all off.

Still totally worth it.

Now it was midday, the sounds of the city echoing through the open balcony.

And I'd just scared my wife half to death.

"What the hell," she whispered, shaking her head. "Why am I like this? I knew you were in the house and coming into the kitchen soon. We were going to eat lunch before we went to visit Shep's old tattoo shop. And yet, I screamed. It's been five years; you would think I'd be okay with this."

Five years since she had been attacked, and everything had changed, five years since we had fallen in love and gotten married. It felt like lifetimes, and just yesterday. And yet, I hated the idea that my wife was still so fricking scared all the time.

"I'm sorry, baby."

"It's not your fault. I just had a weird day. I don't know. You'd think I'd be okay since I never lived in New Orleans when I was on the run, but here I am, acting like a scaredy-cat."

"Does it help that you were defending yourself and looking sexy doing it, or am I just making things worse?" I asked. Considering I was an author and damn good with words, I wasn't making sense.

"Maybe. I don't know. Anyway, I'm making lunch, a few vegetarian options since you're trying to go veggie-saurus with me."

I winced. "We're in New Orleans. I'm going to eat a lot of shellfish. I'm sorry, it's what I do."

"I know, and you're welcome to it, but you're going to let me play while we're in this kitchen."

My brows winged up. "My kind of play or your kind of play?"

She tapped her finger against my chest. "We just had sexy times, and now I'm starving. We're going to eat, have more sexy times in the shower, and go to the tattoo shop to say hi to Shep's friends. We are not getting a tattoo because if we get one outside of Montgomery Ink, your brother and sister will murder us both. Then we're going to walk around and do some reconnaissance work for your next book." She clapped her hands. "Seriously, we have work to do. I cannot wait to read what you do with these characters."

I shook my head. "We also have to meet with my agent because the movie is coming out soon, and they want to do a few press releases."

Autumn beamed. "My favorite little author turned screenwriter turned Oscar-nominated amazing man."

I blushed, shaking my head. "It was an adapted screenplay, and I lost. Let's not forget that I lost last year." While they said it was an honor to be nominated, and it was, I was a little hurt that I hadn't won. I didn't know why, because I hadn't even expected to be nominated, but Autumn had looked fricking amazing in her dress next to me on the red carpet. It had felt like a once-in-a-lifetime thing, and yet, there was already buzz about the next movie that had been released at the Cannes Film Festival and would release nationwide soon.

I still couldn't believe this was my life, but here we were, eating vegetables, hanging out in New Orleans, and making movies.

"My Montgomery, the famous author. Who knew that all those tattoos would look so good in a tux?" She frowned. "Oh wait, that was me. The bad boy writer. Little do they know that you still like to dictate to me while you're in the office, just in case things get a little hard for you."

I threw my head back and laughed. "You're ridiculous. I love you." I reached around, slid my hands up the shirt to grip her ass. Then I spread her slightly to see if she was ready for me.

She narrowed her eyes before I smiled, lifted her up, and wrapped her legs around my waist. We went hard and fast against the table, both of us knowing how each one liked the taste and touch of one another. It was as if we had always been here, had learned each sensation, and never wanted it to end.

When we finally showered, and I started a load of laundry, Autumn finished making lunch. Then we ate it on the balcony as we watched a wedding parade move across the street in front of us.

"It's a Second Line wedding parade. And I'm kind of sad that we didn't get to have one."

"They don't have them in Denver, babe."

"Maybe, but as a wedding signifies the start of a new beginning of life, a wedding here means you get to have a lot more fun than you do up in Denver."

"How about this, when we hit ten years, or even twenty-five years, we'll have a second wedding down in New Orleans."

She beamed. "Let's do ten years, fifteen years we could have one on the beach somewhere, twenty years we can do it at a snow chalet somewhere in the Alps."

I laughed. "And we're bringing all of the Montgomerys when we do? Because I'm going to have to write a few more books and movies for that to happen."

Autumn just cringed. "Sometimes it can just be us. I mean, why not? We're doing pretty good on our own."

"Yeah, we are." She squeezed my hand, and we watched the happy couple make their way down the road.

My phone buzzed, and I looked down at the text, shaking my head at something that Tabby texted.

"What is it?" Autumn asked as she looked over my shoulder. "Oh my God, the twins are too cute. Seriously. I have a list of every single nephew and niece that we have just in case we miss one since they are growing leaps and bounds. I need to start my shopping for them."

"You know they don't need a gift from Uncle Griffin and Aunt Autumn every time we go somewhere. We've been traveling a lot more than usual. We're going to spoil those kids."

Autumn just waved me off. "Of course we are. We're the aunt and uncle. Grandma and Grandpa get to do it too, and this is our thing."

I looked at her then, my heart feeling two times too big. "Are you okay that we're still going to stay aunt and uncle? That we decided that we're better off and happier without making babies of our own?"

Autumn's smile softened. "I like our life. I like the fact that your family is procreating enough for the entire world twice over. We have so many nieces and nephews that are like our own. I don't need a baby for this part of our lives. I never thought I could want to be a mother, not with my life before, and I like the fact that you and I are creating our life. There are so many different ways to grow up and have a family. We're not making do. We're making the family that we want. And spoiling those kids completely without having to deal with every single runny nose or PTA mom, or anything else."

I just shook my head, laughing. "We had to go to the PTA meeting last week for Leif's school. I'm not quite sure what you're talking about there."

Autumn winced. "Fine. We still have to deal with all of that, yet we're living the life we want. I love that we live in a world now that we do not have to have children to feel complete. But we can have so many children in our lives that it feels like we're parents nonetheless. I'm happy, Griffin. Aren't you?" she asked, her voice low.

I leaned over and kissed her softly. "I love our life. Seriously, I never thought I could have something like this. I could have you. But here we are, not making do, but making our life. I'm fucking happy. Now, let's see the rest of the town. I hear there's a vampire tour with our names on it."

Autumn clapped her hands. "Yes. This is what I've been waiting for. I have our schedule for the tours that we're doing. Not just ghost tours, but full-on pagan tours. This is my time." She held up her hands, and I just shook my head, laughing.

"Okay then. Let's get it done. The amount of research that's going into this book might make a whole new series."

Autumn grinned. "That's what I'm talking about. I love you." She leaned forward, kissed me softly, and I beamed up at her.

"I love you too, babe. Now let's go see New Orleans."

Autumn

We ended up at a small café a few hours later, our feet aching from the tours we had already been on, and I just shook my head at the antics of a cute busker. They had a beautiful sound, their voice a deep tenor, and they knew what they were doing with a guitar, but they were currently in the middle of a battle royale with a juggler who sang as well across the street.

I had my phone out, taking a video as I smiled, shaking my head. "I'm going to have to send this to Maya. She's going to love it."

"I hope that she and Jake and Border get to come down here soon."

"I already offered, and I figured that we could watch the kids too."

Griffin nodded, leaning back into the seat. "Of course. It's what we do."

"You sure you're okay with that?" I asked, looking up at him.

He nodded. "Of course. We're always the designated babysitters. This way, we get to hang out with them whenever we want. Or watch them for the week, or pawn them off to one of the many siblings that I have, and then the trio can come down to New Orleans, enjoy themselves. With everything that's been going on, they haven't had enough of a vacation."

I nodded and stopped the video once the juggler held up his hands in triumph.

"I cannot believe the juggler won," Griffin deadpanned, and I grinned.

"It's a skill. One that I cannot do. How do you have so many balls in the air that you can take care of?" Griffin leered at me, and I rolled my eyes. "Are you, like, ten? Yes, I said balls. Balls, balls, balls."

A mother with her two children glared at me as she scurried off, but the drunk man beside us cheered. "Balls!"

"Balls!" a group of revelers added, and the juggler bowed before going back to making a living.

I put my head in my hands, blushing. "Oh, good. So glad that this is what I'll be remembered for."

Griffin pulled my hand away and smiled up at me. "What? I just laughed. You're the one that made it a thing."

"Jerk. I love you."

"Love you too. Now let's go. We have reservations in a couple of hours, and I need to change."

I beamed. "I can't wait to see you in a suit."

"I'm not wearing the jacket."

"That's fine, then I'm not wearing panties," I whispered into his ear, and he groaned.

"You're a very bad woman."

"I am. I can't help it. But then, after dinner, you get to slowly see exactly what else I'm wearing underneath my dress, if anything at all. It's sort of what I do."

"Tempt me?"

"Of course. It's my job to tempt you, to push you, and to love you. I'm your wife, Griffin. I'm here to be your everything. Duh."

"And they say I'm the author, the one with the way with words." He slid his finger down my nose, then kissed me softly as someone cheered behind us. My foot popped as if I was in a rom-com, and I wrapped my arms around his neck, and he did the same around my waist. I ground into him as someone yelled at us to get a room. Another person told us to take it off.

I just laughed into my husband and then took his hand as we walked towards our rental.

"You ever think about living here?" Griffin asked as we made our way underneath the dangling Spanish moss.

"No, with so many years of wandering, I found my home. We can drop everything and travel when we want to, but I like that we'll always have a home. And Denver's it."

He squeezed my hand as we walked up the stairs. "Good. I find Denver's home too. But I want to see the world with you, Autumn. I want to see everything with you."

My heartbeat sped up, and I went up to my toes to kiss his jaw. "Good. Because I can't wait to see the world with you, although I have to say, you are my world."

He laughed, and I cringed. "What? Did I lose the ability to write? You're the author, but I thought I was picking a few things up."

My husband grinned at me. "I don't know. You're going to have to go back to the rough draft on that, maybe do a little editing, a little more dictation."

I couldn't help but snort. "Your lines are getting worse, old man. You better spice it up if you want to keep me."

"I think I can do that."

And then he threw me over his shoulder, and I laughed, and I fell that much more in love with Griffin Montgomery.

Then again, this happened every day.

He was just that much harder to resist. And frankly, I never wanted to.

All About the Veggies

Veggie Lasagna

Tuscan Portobellos

Southwest Pasta Salad

Green Goddess Salad

VEGGIE LASAGNA

15 ounces ricotta cheese

½ cup grated Parmesan cheese

2 tablespoons basil pesto

24 ounces marinara sauce (I use Ragu Simply)

9 "no-boil" lasagna noodles

8 ounces mushrooms, sliced

1 zucchini, thinly sliced

1 squash, thinly sliced

1 onion, thinly sliced

1 eggplant, thinly sliced

2 cups shredded mozzarella cheese

Preheat oven to 350 degrees. In a large bowl, combine the ricotta, Parmesan cheese, and basil pesto. In a 9 x 13-inch baking dish, place about ½ cup of marinara sauce in the bottom of the dish. Top with 3 noodles, 1/3 of the ricotta mixture, a layer of each vegetable and 1/3 of the sauce. Top with ½ cup of mozzarella then repeat the layers 2 more times and top with the remaining 1 cup of mozzarella cheese. Bake for 1 hour. Allow to rest for 10 minutes before slicing.

TUSCAN PORTOBELLOS

6 large portobello mushroom caps
3 tablespoons butter, melted
2 tablespoons Worcestershire sauce
1 tablespoon minced garlic
12 ounces goat cheese, crumbled
1 cup sun-dried tomatoes, chopped
Fresh basil, thinly sliced
Balsamic glaze

Preheat oven to 375 degrees. Using a spoon, gently scrape out the gills of the mushroom caps. Mix together the butter, Worcestershire sauce and garlic. Using a basting brush, coat both sides of each mushroom. Place on a cookie sheet. Stuff each one with equal parts goat cheese and sun dried tomatoes. Bake for 8-10 minutes, then top with fresh basil and balsamic glaze.

QUICK TIP: *Balsamic glaze can be made at home by simply simmering 2 cups of balsamic vinegar with ½ cup dark brown sugar. This usually takes about 8-10 minutes to thicken.*

SOUTHWEST PASTA SALAD

1 bottle ranch dressing (I use Hidden Valley)
1 packet taco seasoning
Juice of 1 lime (about ¼ cup)
1 (16 ounce) box rotini pasta, cooked and cooled
1 (14.5 ounce) can black beans, drained and rinsed
1 (14.5 ounce) can corn, drained
1 red onion, diced
1 cup cherry tomatoes, quartered
2 cups shredded cheddar cheese

In a large bowl, combine the ranch dressing, taco seasoning and lime juice. Add in remaining ingredients and toss to coat. Refrigerate overnight.

GREEN GODDESS SALAD

Dressing
1 avocado, peeled and pitted
1 cup buttermilk
2 tablespoons chopped chives
2 teaspoons white vinegar
1 teaspoon anchovy paste

1 head butter lettuce
1 small cucumber, thinly sliced
1 small can artichoke hearts
1 stalk celery, chopped

In a blender, add all ingredients for the dressing and puree until smooth. Place loosely chopped lettuce in a large bowl, add remaining toppings, and toss with dressing.

CHAPTER 5

With a Twist

Maya

The sun sank into my skin, and I lifted my chin, hoping the rays touched every inch of me showing. Considering I was in a very tiny bikini, there was a decent amount of skin.

"I swear I'm going to put a towel over you if you don't stop preening like that," Border grumbled from my side, and I grinned over at him.

"Aw, you don't like me showing the girls?"

"Woman, you are practically falling out of that bathing suit, one wrong move and the world gets to see your nipples."

Jake, my other wonderfully sweet and growly husband, snorted from my other side. "Border, babe, we are the only three on this part of the beach. Our private beach. I think it's okay that we are enjoying ourselves practically naked. Though I'm quite worried that our wife is wearing anything at all right now."

"I didn't want to have a sunburn on my boobs. There's nothing worse than nipple burn."

The guys looked at me, then down at their shirtless selves. "Really? That's what you're going with?"

I rolled my eyes, then undid the top of my bikini. Both guys groaned, and I just grinned, loving how they looked at me, their gazes hungry.

"Well, I guess this is a decent way to celebrate our anniversary."

"It's not too shabby if I say so myself," Jake added, rolling his shoulders back.

I grinned. "Considering I'm using both of you for your bodies and your money just now, I'm okay with that. A whole vacation where we don't have the kids, I am currently topless on our beach, next to our private villa, and later I'm going to go skinny dipping and screw both of your brains out. I honestly do not see the problem here."

Both men looked at each other over my body, and then Border pounced. I let out a laugh, rolling, so the three of us were tangled limbs, wet mouths, and all heat.

"Well, I'm glad we took that shower because I don't think I'm ever going to get all the sand out of places," Jake said with a laugh as he gingerly walked out of the shower, towel around his hips.

I snorted, shaking my head as I slid on a pair of lace panties and looked at the different flowy dresses that I had brought for our anniversary vacation.

I still couldn't quite believe it had been ten years since I had married my men. Legally, I was only married to one of them, but in reality both of them were my husbands. We all shared the same last name, and they were parents, legally and emotionally, if not biologically, to our four kids.

I slid my hands over my slightly wider-than-they-had-been hips and grinned. Border slid up behind me and wrapped his arms around me, kissing my neck. I smiled, loving the way that his big hulking frame towered over mine. I wasn't small, but he always made me feel it. He was gorgeous, growly, and so damned protective that sometimes it was hard to breathe. But it was his job to be protective, and his security company did well enough for the stars flocking to Colorado for mountain time that we had enough money for an all-inclusive, private, very chic vacation. Between that and Jake's art exploding in recent years, him becoming a hot commodity, we were doing amazingly well for ourselves.

Montgomery Ink was doing just fine as well, with a third and possibly fourth shop opening eventually. We were trying to keep it still in the family, but with only three technical Montgomerys in it, we didn't want to lose our Montgomery flair. Austin and I were making it work, but it was still a little scary sometimes when we weren't exactly sure what we were doing.

"You're getting all worried over there, you okay?" Jake asked as he stepped into his tan shorts.

I looked over at him and then at my shaved-head-of-a-husband, Border, and grinned. "I think I'm doing pretty great. I still can't believe that we're here. I miss our babies."

Border sighed. "Do we want to call them? We could."

I shook my head. "No, my parents and Griffin and Autumn have them safe."

"I still can't believe Noah's almost ten," Jake added. "And Skyler's eight, Cooper is five, and our little Naomi is three. Seriously, it doesn't make any sense. How do we have so many kids that are getting older?"

I laughed and tapped his face with my fingers. "That's what time does. I mean, it's not like we have a kid out of college and working on a family of his own, like a certain brother of mine."

Border laughed behind me as he buttoned up his shirt. "Well, Austin did get started a little early in the family department."

"True. Although I think our generation might be done with having kids at this point."

Jake frowned. "You think? I thought Miranda was going for number four."

I shook my head. "No, I think the fifty-five grandkids that we have so far are enough. Even my cousins are pretty much done having kids. It's time for the next generation."

Border shuddered. "Our baby is three years old. Let's not think about her dating, because if she starts dating someone like Jake and me, we're going to have a problem."

Both of my husbands laughed, and I slid my hands into theirs and squeezed. "I promise I will hold you back from being the growly dads that we hate. The overprotective ones that don't make any sense because our kids aren't our property."

Border and Jake gave each other looks. "And we promise we'll do the same to you," Jake added, and I flipped him off lovingly.

"Deal. Now, let's go out and get some food. I'm craving fresh fish or steak. I don't know. We'll just have to get three different meals so I can have them all," I added.

Border smirked. "It's an all-inclusive. We can have as much as we want, and I swear I will feed you all night if I have to."

"Aw, that's sweet. I've never been the eat a single piece of lettuce for dinner type of girl."

"Good, because I don't know if I'd recognize you if you were." Jake's mouth ravaged mine, and his hand slid up my dress and squeezed my ass. I groaned, then pulled away.

"I'm hungry, no sex until later. We just had beach sex."

"Yes, and sand-burn is a thing," Jake added with a laugh, and I shook my head and followed my men out of our private villa and to the restaurant area. I still didn't know how I'd gotten this lucky, to find two men who not only loved me but each other. It wasn't easy, but it was our life, and I would forever be grateful for the time that I fell for them. And they fell right back.

Border

We sat at the steakhouse part of the all-inclusive, where we did indeed get a steak, a big pork chop of some sort, a roasted chicken, and the fish for our girl.

Maya practically danced in her seat, humming as she went to town on our dinners, and I laughed, my stomach filling up with the indulgent food.

Maya was sexy most days just breathing, but when she was happy and full and not giving a shit about what the world thought? That was the woman that I loved.

Jake sat on my other side, leaning back into his chair with his hands on his stomach. "I think I overate," he growled, his eyes closed. "Border, babe, why did you let me do too much?"

I reached out, squeezed his knee, and grinned. "I'm never going to tell you to stop doing something, because then you'd do it even more. I know you, husband of mine."

It was nice to be at a place where there were only a few other couples, the resort inclusive enough that we didn't feel like we had to hide who we were. Sometimes we did our best not to showcase that we were a poly relationship that was long-term and raising kids. It wasn't that we hid. It was just easier emotionally not to flaunt ourselves. Just like I wouldn't make out with Maya on one of our single dates on a table, I wasn't going to do the same with both of my spouses. It just made sense to act like we normally did, without having sex in front of strangers.

But still, it was nice to have the casual touches, to be with one another and just hang out.

"I know that we're all stuffed, but tomorrow we're going to that twisty place."

I frowned at Maya's words. "Twisty?"

"The place called With A Twist. Every food has a twist to it. Like pizzas, grilled cheeses, just a play on words. We are our own twisted relationship; I thought it'd be cute." She fluttered her eyes, and I looked down at the martini in her hands.

"How many of those have you had?"

"Well, it's a martini with a twist, so that will tell you my answer," she added, draining the rest of her glass.

I laughed, took the empty glass from her, and then kissed her softly on the mouth. "Well then, that sounds like a very nice plan to me."

"I could eat," Jake added, leaning forward.

"You just said you were full," Maya laughed.

"I didn't tell you what I wanted my dessert to be." He lowered his voice, leaning forward, his molten gaze on Maya and me. My shorts were oddly tight just then, and I swallowed hard.

"Well, I guess we have to go back to our room to make sure we take care of your dessert needs."

Jake leaned forward, kissed me softly, then did the same to Maya.

"I cannot believe you would just do that so flagrantly out in the open," a woman with a short haircut and narrowed eyes snapped as she walked by. "There could have been children here. And you're out showcasing, what? That you think it's cool to go to hell? You're living in sin. What kind of perverted things are you doing to each other? I cannot believe I have to share the same restaurant with you. Well, no bother, with the tattoos and piercings you have, you clearly have a friend who got you in or had a coupon or something. I don't know what the hell this place is thinking, letting your kind in, but I will be speaking to the manager." She raised her chin and stomped off, her high heels grating.

And just like that, my mood soured.

Maya was just on the edge of drunk that her eyes filled instead of going to anger. And that broke me. My wife did not cry. She did not weep or get emotional or turn on us when things got hard. She got angry, she got determined, and she got shit done.

But that bitch had made my wife cry. I pushed my seat back, but then Jake squeezed my hand. "No, let's not."

"We're going to let her talk to us like that?"

Maya met my gaze. "Let's just go back to the room. People are staring. They were already staring earlier, with the tattoos and the three of us at a couple's place. I'm kind of over it."

Ten years. Ten years of us being together and sometimes dealing with this, I truly hadn't expected it now. Being in a poly relationship was boring these days. There were celebrity couples in poly triads, where co-parenting over two sets of kids was a thing. It was the norm.

But maybe it was still too "dirty" for people who had once thought themselves the average and pristine.

I sighed and then got up from the table. "Come on. I was promised dessert."

Neither Jake nor Maya looked in the mood for it anymore, so that meant I'd be ordering cake to the room and cuddling my spouses.

I hadn't said anything to that woman, and I should have. I should have stood up for the people that I loved, but I hadn't.

So tonight, I would care for the people that I loved. I'd find a way to make it better.

It seemed like it was the only thing I could do.

Jake

The next morning I had a headache, probably because of way too much vodka, and Maya was still sleeping, wrapped around Border. Border had gone to bed sober, anger settling into his bones, and there was nothing I could do to fix it.

We were used to people being outright rude and snarly to us. The fact that it had come as a surprise yesterday was what had hurt. Because we hadn't been expecting it, and we hadn't been on edge like we always were, for either the tattoos, the piercings, the fact that we were a triad. It was even worse at first when we were at PTA meetings for our eldest, the three of us, a unit as a parental team, and some people not understanding. Noah had gone to three different schools until we found something perfect for him. One where he was never bullied for who he was and who his parents were. Now all three kids would be going to that school, and they wouldn't even be the only kids with a poly set of parents.

Families were made up of a rainbow of groupings and circumstances, and their school understood that.

The fact that we had to pay an astronomical amount to go there notwithstanding.

I let them sleep, left a note, and went for a walk. I needed to breathe. I had a few art pieces that were due soon, a few shows coming up, even one European tour on the way. My life was completely different than it had once been, and I was okay with that. I just hated that the same bigotry kept showing up, even when we changed.

The beach was quiet, the sun just rising as I made my way towards the center of the resort. I hadn't even realized I was going there until I found myself in front of the central area. The staff was working, waved, and smiled at me, and I nodded at them, knowing they would stop everything to help me, and while I appreciated that, I didn't want to cut into their day. They were working their asses off to help us, just like they were helping the douche bags that we had seen last night. So I would not get in their way.

"Mr. Montgomery-Gallagher?" a voice said from behind me, and I turned.

"Oh. Hello, Mr. Loredo."

"Call me Theo," the other man corrected. "I was going to come and see you and your spouses later today, but since you're here, why don't we go for a little walk?"

My shoulders tensed. If they kicked us out because they figured out who we were or what we did in our private time, I was going to blow a gasket. There were many ways they could get around certain bigotry laws, and those laws didn't necessarily extend to where we were anyway.

The other man's gaze narrowed. "Before you go with me, I guess I should apologize."

My shoulders fell, and I blinked. "What?"

"Come, let's go for a walk away from listening ears."

"Oh, I guess. Yeah, sure." Confused, I followed the other man as we walked on the beach, the manager's white slacks billowing in the slight breeze.

"My grandfather built this resort when my father was still a kid."

"Oh?"

"Yes. And then eventually I became manager and owner."

"Oh, I didn't realize you were the owner."

"I try not to let everyone know that, because then some people get a little weird about who I am and what I own."

"I get you. Sometimes you just want to be seen for yourself and not for the circumstances surrounding you."

"Good, you found my not-so-subtle train of thought." Theo sighed. "I am sorry for what happened last night. I didn't hear about it until the three of you had already left, and I didn't want to interrupt your night. However, just know the matter has been taken care of."

I stopped, the sound of the waves crashing filling my ears. "What do you mean?"

"The woman and her husband will no longer be welcome at any of my resorts or the chain of resorts that are within my community."

I blinked, stunned and confused. "Wait. What? I don't understand."

"I have friends in high places; it's what I do. And my friends and I are of a like mind that people with certain attitudes don't need to be here. They don't need to be part of our circles. To be blunt, Mr. Montgomery-Gallagher—"

"Call me Jake. Our last name is a mouthful."

The other man's lips twitched. "Okay, to be blunt, Jake, I have a lot of money. I make a lot of money. My friends make even more. That couple will no longer be welcome to any of their favorite places because we don't need their money. We don't need them. They can tell their bigoted friends what their feelings are, and they can try to sue, but we don't care because they will never win. I can't take away their words or the pain that they may have caused you, but what I can do is make sure that anything that my name touches won't have them hurt you. My husband and I, as well as our wife and her girlfriend, all agree."

I blinked, trying to come to terms with that information. All of that information.

"You're serious."

Theo just shrugged. "We're living in an age where people are finally able to begin to figure out who they are and be free with who they love. I'm a very blessed man, and my job, my goal in life, is to make sure others can find ways to be equally as blessed. Please tell your spouses that we truly appreciate them, and your stay is on us."

I sputtered. "You don't have to do that. Seriously."

"Seriously," he said sarcastically. "It's on us."

"I don't know what to say."

"Just love your family, be the good people that you are. Because my wife loves your work, and your husband protected my husband from a security threat when we were in Vale. I don't even think Border understands who he was protecting, but he was protecting my heart. So I'm going to do my best to protect yours."

And with that, the other man walked away, and I stood there, confused and wondering how the hell I was going to explain this to my spouses without feeling like I had just woken from a dream.

In the end, I fed my wife pancakes, and her eyes widened as I explained everything.

Border shook his head. "I know that man. I mean, it didn't click that it was the same owner/manager here. Why didn't it? I'm better than that."

"I have a feeling that there are many more secrets than the owner of this resort has up his sleeves, and I want to know them all," Maya added with a laugh.

I shook my head, looked at the loves of my life, and let out a breath. "We are going to be tipping this entire staff a lot. I mean, they had to deal with that woman, and since we're not paying for this trip apparently, let's make sure that the staff knows that we appreciate them."

Border laughed. "Sounds like a plan to me. Now, let's call the kids, see what we've missed in the past however many hours since we spoke to them, because we know it's probably been everything according to Naomi," he added with a laugh. "And then, I'm sensing the need to skinny dip. I want to see my wife naked under the sunlight in the crystal blue waters."

Maya scoffed, but beamed.

"What about me? You don't want to see me naked?"

"If I have to," Border laughed, and then I put the plate down and straddled him.

"Okay, just for that, I'm not going down on you for the next three days."

"Liar," Maya added with a laugh as she pulled me back. We sat in a tangle of limbs, fully clothed since we were about to video call the kids.

I hadn't meant to fall in love with my best friend and my ex-boyfriend, but somehow, they found me. And as the time moved on, I promised myself once again I would never let them go.

And I honestly couldn't wait to see what we did next.

With a Twist

Cheeseburger Spring Rolls

Reuben Quesadillas

Chili Cheese Waffles

Spicy Pop Tarts

Cheesesteak Stuffed Peppers

Eggroll Lettuce Wraps

CHEESEBURGER SPRING ROLLS

1 pound ground beef
1 sweet onion, diced
½ cup dill pickle, diced
1 (8 ounce) block Velveeta cheese, cubed
1 tablespoon Dijon mustard
1 teaspoon Worcestershire sauce
1 package spring roll wrappers
2 cups oil, for frying

In a medium skillet over medium heat, cook ground beef and drain. Return to skillet and add in onion, dill pickle, Velveeta cheese, Dijon mustard, and Worcestershire sauce. Stir over low heat until cheese is melted. Lay a spring roll wrapper flat in a diamond shape. Add 2-3 tablespoons of cheeseburger filling towards the bottom of the wrapper. Roll the wrapper by first folding up the bottom corner towards the top then pull in the sides and roll up. Place a few drops of water on the top corner and finish rolling to seal. Fill a deep fryer or Dutch oven with oil and heat to 350 degrees. Place 2-3 rolls into oil and fry for 1-2 minutes on each side or until golden brown. Remove from oil and place on a plate lined with paper towels.

REUBEN QUESADILLAS

4 flour tortillas
1 cup Thousand Island dressing
8 slices deli corned beef
8 slices swiss cheese
1 cup sauerkraut, drained

Lay out tortillas and spread dressing over entire surface. Place 2 pieces of corned beef on the bottom half of each tortilla. Top with swiss cheese and about 2-3 tablespoons of sauerkraut. Fold tortilla over the filling. In a medium skillet over medium heat, spray with nonstick spray and place quesadilla in skillet. Brown for 1-2 minutes, then spray exposed tortilla and flip to brown other side. Cook for an additional 1-2 minutes. Serve with remaining dressing.

CHILI CHEESE WAFFLES

Waffles

1 cup self-rising flour

1 cup yellow cornmeal

1 teaspoon salt

2 cups milk

2 eggs

⅓ cup butter, melted

2 cups shredded sharp cheddar cheese

In a large bowl, whisk together all ingredients. Heat and grease waffle maker. Add about ½ cup of batter to waffle maker. Cook until brown on both sides. Repeat with remaining batter.

Chili

1 pound ground beef

1 onion, chopped

2 (14.5 ounce) cans chili beans

1 (14.5 ounce) can diced tomatoes

1 (14.5 ounce) can tomato sauce

3 tablespoons chili powder

1 teaspoon ground cumin

1 teaspoon paprika

1 teaspoon salt

1 teaspoon pepper

1 cup sharp cheddar cheese, grated (for garnish)
Sour cream (for garnish)

In a large skillet over medium heat, cook ground beef and onion until beef is cooked through. Drain and place in a large pot or slow cooker. Add in remaining ingredients and stir until well combined. Simmer on low for at least 2 hours before serving. Serve over waffles and top with sour cream and cheese.

QUICK TIP: *If you like your chili a little spicier then add 1 teaspoon of cayenne pepper.*

SPICY POP TARTS

5 jalapeños, diced
1 (8 ounce) block cream cheese
2 cups shredded pepper jack cheese
¼ cup mayonnaise
1 cup bacon pieces
1 egg (egg wash)
1 package puff pastry (2 sheets)

Preheat oven to 400 degrees. In a large bowl, mix together all ingredients except the puff pastry. Line a cookie sheet with parchment paper. Place puff pastry on a lightly floured surface. Using a pastry cutter or knife, cut nine 3-inch by 2-inch rectangles on each sheet, totaling 18 rectangles. Place 1 tablespoon of filling in the center of 9 rectangles. Space the remaining 9 rectangles on top of the filling. Seal the 4 sides with a fork. Brush the top with egg wash and bake for 15 minutes or until golden brown.

QUICK TIP: *Now that you know the basics of how to make a homemade pop tart, get creative! The possibilities are endless.*

CHEESESTEAK STUFFED PEPPERS

4 green bell peppers, halved from top to bottom

½ cup mayonnaise

1 tablespoon butter

1 onion, thinly sliced

1 (16 ounce) package button mushrooms, thinly sliced

1 pound sirloin steak, thinly sliced

1 tablespoon soy sauce

16 slices provolone cheese

Preheat oven to 350 degrees. Place peppers in a 9 x 13-inch baking dish. Brush the inside of each pepper with mayonnaise. In a large skillet over medium heat, cook the onions and mushrooms in the butter. Allow to simmer for about 8-10 minutes, then add in the steak and soy sauce. Cook for an additional 3-5 minutes, then remove from heat. Place one slice of provolone in the bottom of each bell pepper. Fill bell pepper with steak mixture and top with remaining cheese. Bake for 30 minutes.

EGGROLL LETTUCE WRAPS

1 pound ground beef
1 small onion, diced
1 teaspoon minced garlic
1 small head of cabbage, thinly sliced
½ red cabbage, thinly sliced
½ cup julienned carrots
¼ cup soy sauce
2 tablespoons honey
1 head butter lettuce
1 bag tortilla strips

In a large skillet over medium heat, brown ground beef, onions, and garlic until beef is cooked through. Drain and return to skillet over low heat. Add in cabbage, carrots, soy sauce and honey. Stir to combine and cook for 3-5 minutes or until cabbage is tender. Pull apart the lettuce leaves and place on a platter. Add about ¼ cup of filling to each leaf. Top with tortilla strips.

CHAPTER 6

Cheese Me Baby

Tabby

I closed my planner and told myself I would be fine not looking at it for the next hour or so. I could even perhaps take an entire evening off from staring at it.

I held back a snort to that. Oh no, that wouldn't be happening. Not when my entire life was in that planner. Sure, it might be backed up digitally, and I could most likely recite nearly all of it off the top of my head, but I still wanted my paper planner. It was my life, and I loved it.

Maybe not as much as my husband and my children, but that was beside the point.

I slid my chair back from my desk and looked over Montgomery Inc.

When I had come to work here, I had been fresh out of college, a little afraid, and far quieter than I was now. Yes, my three older brothers were fantastic and had never made me feel like anything less, but it was hard to keep up with them sometimes. Only now, as an adult, was I able to speak above their growly and loud voices. They were the best big brothers I could ever ask for, and I hated that they lived so far away.

I bit my lip, then opened my planner again to jot down a note to see when I could go and visit. Or maybe they could come out here. It was easier for Alexander and me, along with the four kids, to make our way out there, versus three brothers, their wives, and their numerous children to come up here.

We'd make it work, though, because I missed my family.

"Tabitha? What's wrong?"

I looked at my husband and smiled. "Just thinking about a trip to Pennsylvania." I closed the top of my planner.

Alexander's brows rose. "It's cold there."

71

I snorted. "We live in Denver. It's not like it's hot here right now. It's winter. Plus, I thought we could go there in summer."

"And then it's humid."

I rolled my eyes calmly and moved around the desk, then went to my tiptoes. I pressed my lips to his and moaned into him, loving the way that he bent down for me so I could reach him.

He smelled a little of sweat and of his aftershave. He shaved off his beard a couple of days ago and kept his face clean skinned. I loved the fact that I could see the strong line of his jaw, but I did miss his beard. Especially the way it felt against me.

"You're moaning, and my brothers could come around the corner any minute. Watch yourself, baby."

I sighed. "Sorry, just thinking about your beard."

My husband grinned, running his hand over his face. "I have a match coming up and wanted it out of the way so the guy couldn't pull it."

I shivered. "I know it's very sexy when you're out there boxing like that, but I still freak out when someone's hitting you."

"This is why I'm at the amateur level where it's a bunch of old guys hitting each other, but not too painfully. I promise I'm not going to break anything."

I quickly knocked on my desk, scowling. "Knock on wood, Alexander Montgomery." He did the same, and I shook my head. "We need to go pick up the kids."

"They should be done with school soon, right?"

I frowned, wondering why he sounded like that. Alexander picked up the kids from school on his own most days, since his schedule was a lot more flexible than mine, but he'd been off recently, and it worried me.

"What's wrong?"

"Nothing, just thinking. And yes, it's time to pick up the kids. You said you were off for a bit and wanted to come with me?"

"I am. It's just the six of us for the rest of the weekend."

"Go have fun," Wes, Alexander's eldest brother, said as he came around the back. "We can handle this without Tabby."

I rolled my eyes and picked up my planner. "We both know that's not true."

Wes grinned, leaned down, and kissed my cheek.

"Watch your hand," Alexander scowled, and Wes just rolled his eyes as his wife Jillian came around, with something that I hoped was dirt on her face. Considering she was a plumber, I didn't want to know.

"Hey, I'd tell your wife to watch her hands, but I'm not a jealous freak like you," Jillian added with a grin.

Alexander rolled his eyes, and I leaned into my husband's side. "We're off to pick up the kids. Are you two good with yours?" Wes and Jillian had three children that were all around the same age as ours.

"We're good. We have to go out to the job sites today, though."

"Okay, just let us know if you need anything."

"You're taking your vacation. Enjoy it," Wes ordered. "I don't want to see that planner anywhere near here."

I clutched my planner to my chest. "How dare you mock my planner? You could hurt his feelings."

Wes rolled his eyes as Jillian just beamed. "Have fun. And eat lots of cheese for us."

"Ooh, now I want cheese," Wes grumbled, rubbing his stomach.

I shook my head and then made my way out to the parking lot.

"I'll follow you to the school?"

"Sounds like a plan."

I hopped into my SUV as Alexander got in his, and we made our way to the elementary school to pick up the kids. Sebastian and Aria were twins and in the fifth grade, while Gus and Dara were twins in the third grade. How I had ended up with two sets of twins, I would never know. Although I suppose twins did run in the family, as Wes was a twin himself, but I still couldn't believe I had two sets.

Remembering the New Year's holiday I had spent with Alexander when I had told him we were pregnant with the second set, I couldn't help but grin. Alexander had been through hell and back, had nearly lost himself, and I had nearly lost him because of his demons and his love of his family. Now we were a big family of our own, and I almost couldn't keep up.

The school line was long, and usually we wouldn't take up the space of two cars, but today was special. And we could explain to the kids why we would both be picking them up.

Sebastian and Aria split up, Aria coming to my car while Sebastian jumped into Alexander's. Then Gus jumped into the back of mine while Dara joined Alexander. It wasn't guys against girls, far from it, but I did like the fact that our kids constantly made sure that everybody got to hang out with each other. Yes, it was loud, yes there was some fighting and brawling and normal sibling rivalries, but my kids were sweet, amazing, and I honestly could not believe that this was my life.

By the time we got home, my head ached from Gus's full rendition of the entire day, and I just shook my head as Aria added a few bits and pieces of hers. Gus chatted a mile a minute, barely letting Aria speak, but my daughter didn't mind. She loved her baby brother with all of her heart, and even though they were close in age, sometimes I felt like they were closer than they were with their respective twins, and the same was true with Dara and Sebastian.

By the time we got inside, unpacked schoolbags, got rid of uneaten sandwiches that should have been eaten, and washed up for a snack, Alexander was already in the kitchen, making a cheese plate. When charcuterie boards had been all the rage, we were already a few years ahead in our love of them. Now we did a weekly spread, usually on the weekends, but since it was the first day of vacation, we had both decided to get started a little early. That meant today was a bright, big board filled with meats and cheeses that made my mouth water. We also had a side of Fried Cheese Curds, a recipe our friend from Wisconsin had sent one year and couldn't live without.

"Tomorrow, I figured we'd do a dessert board, possibly with cheese as well because hello, cheese is life."

When I had married into the Montgomerys, I had known that they loved their cheeses. It wasn't until I had become a full-fledged Montgomery that I realized that it was true, cheese was their life, and there was no stopping it.

You either loved cheese, or you found a way to share your pieces so you could have something else.

"This looks amazing." I took a picture of it, sent it to the family group chat mostly because Alexander was an artist with it, and while we didn't try to one-up each other with our boards, it was nice to get ideas. The group chat immediately exploded with thumbs up or comments, mostly making fun of my husband from his brothers, just because they could. The fact that they felt comfortable enough to play with Alexander the way that they had before everything had changed made something melt inside of me. They had been so careful with Alexander for so long because of his addiction. It was as if they hadn't known what to say or who the person in front of them now was without the anger constantly plaguing Alexander's soul and speech.

But now, things were different. We were different. We were whole. Happy. Although he was still brooding sometimes. More so recently than usual, and that worried me. But maybe once the kids were asleep, I would pry it out of him. I would have to use some form of cheese to make it work.

"Okay, time to eat," Alexander added with a clap of his hands. We went through the motions of washing the kids' hands, making sure they were all ready, and then we sat down in the living room all spread around the coffee table, and we ate to our hearts' contents. With the addition of some fruits and veggies to the board, it was a full meal, even if it might've been considered just a snack.

We put on a Marvel movie as Alexander went through all of the theories and explanations for each and every cameo and foreshadowing.

I just shook my head, then snuck out my notebook to write the ones that I had missed before. We had Montgomery dinners where we would watch Marvel movies and try to figure out what was coming next or who we thought the bad guy was and had been doing it for years. I was still catching up, as I hadn't been a fan of comics when I was younger, but now I needed to try to beat some of my nieces and nephews at the game. Apparently, being a Montgomery meant you were competitive.

When I went into the kitchen to clean up, the kids spread out while watching a movie. Alexander followed me, a frown on his face.

I turned to him, set the cutting board down, and dried off my hands. "Do you want to tell me what's wrong?"

He bit his lip and worry filled me. "What's wrong, Alexander? Do you need to go to a meeting?"

We had started off our marriage knowing that I would plainly ask without going around him if I was worried about his sobriety. And he would not be offended if I was worried because we both knew that Alexander was an alcoholic. He would be an alcoholic forever, and I was the supportive wife who understood that and knew he would be fighting his addiction forever, even if the tones of his addiction changed over time.

Alexander cursed under his breath and came to my side, cupping my face. He kissed me softly, and I moaned into him. "I'm okay. It's not that. I'm sorry for worrying you."

I cringed. "Are you sure? I can stay here with the kids."

"I don't want to drink right now. I promise you. It's a good thing. I'm just . . . I just need to be out with it."

I blinked. "Be out with what?" I asked cautiously.

"I just got an offer for a job."

I reared back. "Really? Where?"

"Christian Toro Fashion Design."

I blinked. "Fashion? Wait, Christian Toro?" My hands went to my face. "Oh my God, that's brilliant. Didn't we just read that he was looking for a new in-house photographer?"

"Not that job. No, this one is for high-end fashion, celebrity couture, and part of their charity base. Including building a foundation to help recovering addicts and their families. He wants to make a book, and he wants my photography to be part of it." He went into the job details, and then when he named the starting salary, I blinked. "That...that's seven figures."

"For the project, Tabitha. The project alone, let alone the additional projects that come from that. I mean, I made a decent amount over time with my books, and I do very well for myself, enough so that the kids never have to worry about college, and we paid off our house and are thinking about a cabin in Vail, but this is different."

"Alexander. Wait, would you have to live there? In New York?" My heart twisted. His family was here. My new family was here. The children had been born here, and my job was here. Everything was here. But I would move. For Alexander, I would move.

He shook his head, pushed my hair from my face. "A lot of it will be up in Vail. I'll have to go into New York often, but apparently he has a private jet to make sure I can get there on time."

I blinked back, staggering. "There's got to be thousands of photographers in New York, Alexander. I mean, why would he want you to stay here?"

"I'm going to take that as not questioning my prowess," he added, and I flinched.

"Alexander."

"Sorry, yes, there are a thousand different people he could have picked, but he picked me. He wants my eye, not just to take photos for a magazine, but for something important, for his brand, for the charity, and for the foundation that he's building. It isn't what I usually do, but the ideas that he has? I'm excited. And we wouldn't have to move. This is a big thing for us."

I went to my tiptoes and kissed him hard. "I say we bring out the sparkling cider, and we celebrate."

"I love you, Tabitha," he whispered, and I kissed him hard again.

"I love you, Montgomery. Always."

Alex

As I finished packing for my trip, my hands went clammy. I didn't need to drink. I didn't want to. I had gone to a meeting earlier, so my sponsor knew where I was. I'd been an addict for over a decade, been in the program for just as long, and I was sober. However, this big change and the constant flying back and forth that was coming up were going to be difficult. Christian Toro was also a recovering alcoholic and drug addict. However, he was open with his sobriety and his path to being clean. I had to think that perhaps that was one reason we had connected the way we had for the job. I wasn't sure, but in the end, it didn't matter.

All that did matter was that he wasn't going to want me to drink, and I wasn't going to want to either.

"Okay, kids, dinner's ready!" Tabitha called from the kitchen. I zipped up my suitcase, set it back on the ground, then made my way into the kitchen. The kids were piled around the kitchen table as I went around the stove and wrapped my arms around Tabitha's waist. I kissed her neck, and she shivered before patting me away. "Stop it. Behave."

"Never." I winked as I said it, the excitement of the upcoming trip buzzing through the air. Since winter vacation was coming up soon, the kids and Tabitha would join me in New York for a whole week so they could see the Christmas tree and New York in the holiday season. I still didn't know what I was doing sometimes, but with the excitement on their faces, the look in their gazes, I figured I was doing a good job.

"The kids already set the table, now for your good luck and goodbye dinner, it's just us." She kissed me hard on the mouth, and then I took the platter from her.

I groaned as I looked down at the cheesy concoction in front of me.

"I love you."

"I know, husband of mine."

I set the Steak and Cheddar Melt on the table, and the kids clapped and cheered. As I sat down next to Tabitha, my arm around her shoulders, we dug in, and I grinned.

This job was going to change everything, and it meant that a lot of the next few months were going to ride on Tabitha's shoulders at home, but the Montgomerys had a nanny just for this purpose. With so many kids being born, the family took care of each other, and there was a team to make sure that Tabitha wasn't doing everything alone. I'd be home more often than not, with this New York trip being the longest since it was the start. And we were going to make it work. I was doing what I loved. I was clean, happy, and the most blessed man in the world.

And with the cheese in front of us, the kids currently fighting over their favorite cheeses, I just shook my head—once a Montgomery, always a Montgomery. But in the end, cheese was life.

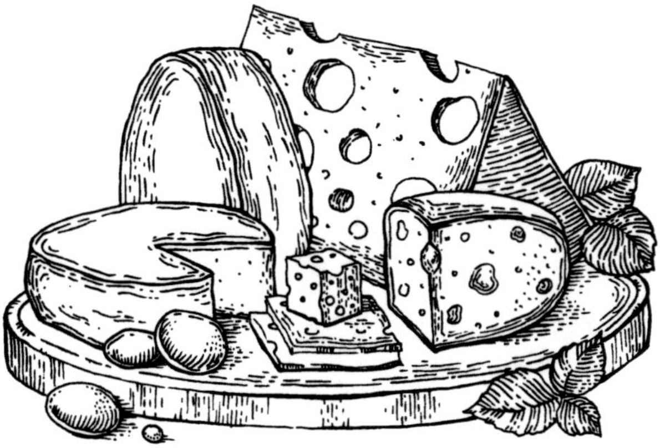

Cheese Me, Baby

Cheesy Chicken Enchiladas

French Toast Grilled Cheese with Bacon

3-Cheese Hashbrown Casserole

Fried Cheese Curds

Broccoli Cheese Soup

Steak and Cheddar Melt

CHEESY CHICKEN ENCHILADAS

2 cups shredded chicken (I use a rotisserie chicken)//
2 cups shredded Monterey jack cheese//
1 packet taco seasoning//
1 (4 ounce) can green chiles, drained//
1 cup sour cream//
10 taco-sized flour tortillas//
1 container white cheese dip//
½ cup milk

Preheat oven to 350 degrees. In a large bowl, combine chicken, Monterey jack cheese, taco seasoning, green chiles and sour cream. Place about ½ cup of the mixture in the middle of each tortilla and roll up, placing seam side down in a 9 x 13-inch baking dish. In a small pot over low heat, combine the cheese dip and milk. Stir on low until melted. Pour over the enchiladas and bake for 20-25 minutes.

FRENCH TOAST GRILLED CHEESE WITH BACON

6 eggs

½ cup milk

½ teaspoon salt

1 teaspoon sugar

16 slices sharp cheddar cheese

16 slices bacon, cooked and cut in half

8 slices Texas toast (or your favorite thick-sliced bread)

2 tablespoons butter

Maple syrup

In a large bowl, whisk together eggs, milk, salt, and sugar. Top 4 slices of toast with 1 slice cheddar cheese, 4 half pieces of bacon, then another slice of cheddar cheese. Top with remaining toast. Dip each sandwich in the egg mixture, making sure to coat both sides. In a large skillet over low heat, melt ½ tablespoon of butter and place one sandwich in skillet. Brown each side of sandwich for 3-4 minutes. Remove from skillet and repeat with remaining sandwiches. Serve with maple syrup.

3-CHEESE HASHBROWN CASSEROLE

1 bag frozen shredded hash browns

⅓ cup butter melted

1 teaspoon salt

1 teaspoon pepper

1 onion, diced

1 can cream of chicken soup

1 cup sharp cheddar cheese

1 cup Colby jack cheese

1 cup mozzarella cheese

Preheat oven to 375 degrees. In a large bowl, mix together all ingredients. Pour into a 9 x 13-inch baking dish and bake uncovered for 45 minutes.

FRIED CHEESE CURDS

2-3 cups oil, for frying

1 cup self-rising flour

½ teaspoon salt

2 eggs

½ cup milk

1 pound cheese curds

Heat oil to 350 degrees in a deep fryer or Dutch oven. In a medium bowl, whisk together flour, salt, eggs, and milk until mixture is smooth. Coat cheese curds in batter and fry 3-4 at a time for 1 minute. Remove and place on a paper towel-lined plate.

BROCCOLI CHEESE SOUP

6 tablespoons butter

1 onion, diced

¼ cup all-purpose flour

2 cups vegetable broth

2 cups heavy cream

3 cups broccoli, cut into bite-sized pieces

1 teaspoon salt

1 teaspoon pepper

1 cup shredded sharp cheddar cheese

In a medium skillet over medium heat, add 2 tablespoons butter and onion. Cook for 8-10 minutes. In a large stockpot, add remaining 4 tablespoons butter and ¼ cup flour. Stir constantly for about 2-3 minutes to form a roux. Slowly add in vegetable broth, stirring constantly, then add in heavy cream slowly, also constantly stirring. Simmer for 20 minutes, then add in the broccoli, salt and pepper. Simmer for an additional 20 minutes. Stir in cheese and cook for 1-2 more minutes. Remove from heat and serve.

STEAK AND CHEDDAR MELT

1 cup thinly sliced red onions
½ cup white vinegar
1 tablespoon sugar
1 tablespoon butter
1 (14-16 ounce) sirloin steak
1 teaspoon salt
1 teaspoon pepper
½ cup mayonnaise
4 tablespoons horseradish
4 hoagie rolls
8 slices sharp white cheddar cheese

To make pickled onions, place onions, vinegar, and sugar in a small pot over medium heat and bring to a boil. Boil for 3-5 minutes until onions are tender. Remove from heat and allow to cool in pickling liquid. Bring the sirloin steak to room temperature and season with salt and pepper. In a large iron skillet over high heat, add butter and sear the steak for 2-3 minutes on both sides for medium rare. Remove from heat and allow to rest for 10 minutes. Thinly slice steak. In a small bowl, mix together mayonnaise and horseradish and spread on inside of hoagie rolls. Top with 4-5 slices of steak, 2-3 tablespoons of pickled onions, and 2 slices of cheddar cheese. Broil for 3-5 minutes or until cheese is melted.

CHAPTER 7

Call Me Cupcake

Storm

My sister-in-law was the planner. Not me. Wes, my twin brother, was the planner. Again, not me. And yet, I wasn't about to cave. I would do this. I would probably make mistakes, end up a little messy, but as long as I made Everly smile, that was all that mattered.

"What do you mean you don't have the cake?" I asked the baker in front of me, my eyes wide.

I should have gone with Hailey, the owner of Taboo, but she was busy with her kids, her business, and frankly, she wasn't a baker. She was a business owner, did some baking, and was a barista at the café, but she didn't bake cakes for functions like this. I hadn't wanted to bother her since she hadn't been feeling well, so I had hired someone that a friend of ours had used.

I should have used my damn cousin down in Colorado Springs who owned a freaking bakery, or even one of my cousin-in-law's wife's bakeries. There were so many baked goods within the Montgomerys it was ridiculous, yet I had hired a practical stranger to get it done, and it wasn't getting done.

"I'm sorry, Mr. Montgomery. I truly am. But you talked to my assistant, not me. I should say, my former assistant. I will do whatever I can to try to get this done for you, but honestly, a cake for over one hundred people just isn't going to happen for tonight. I'm sorry."

The woman raised her chin and didn't look sorry in the least. Not only was her former assistant incompetent, but this woman also didn't seem to understand that I was out of my depth here and failing.

All I wanted was to do one not kid-friendly surprise party for my wife. A birthday party-slash-anniversary party for the new bookstore, where the kids would be with babysitters, and the adults in our family and friends group could just enjoy themselves without two thousand kids running around. There was going to be cheese, alcohol, non-alcoholic drinks for those who didn't drink, seared meat of some sort that I was excited about from the caterer, and a goddamn cake from this place.

But apparently, we weren't getting a cake.

"This is unacceptable. I called to confirm."

"I don't know what to tell you or who you talked to, but that wasn't us. Mr. Montgomery, I have a lot to do, and while I would love to help, I can't."

So much for doing all in their power to make sure I could get it. It looked like they weren't going to do a fucking thing. No, I was fucking screwed, and it was only my word against theirs. I had an email, I had a confirmation, and now I had a check from them for the down payment since I was getting a refund.

I needed to scream.

"Again, I'm sorry, but I have to go, and you need to leave."

"I'll go, but I'll make sure that none of my family uses you."

"I'm sure you could use any one of your family members, Mr. Montgomery. Perhaps your brother-in-law's place? What is Jake doing these days?"

She smirked as she said it before she turned on her heel and left.

I was going to kill my brother-in-law. Kill him.

It had been what, ten years since he'd been married to Maya and Border, and yet another ex-girlfriend was coming out of the woodwork. Yes, Jake's ex-girlfriend Holly was a family friend and was even coming to the fricking surprise party that was going to be without a cake, but it seemed Jake had another ex.

My hands shook as I dialed the phone and called the other man.

"Hey there, Storm. You getting ready for tonight?"

"I'm going to kill you. I'm going to deck you. Just you wait."

Jake cleared his throat. "You sound a little bit more like Wes, or even Austin. Are you sure this is Storm Montgomery? What did I do?"

"You slept with a woman named Francesca at some point over ten years ago and screwed with her because now I'm not getting the damn cake for tonight." I was three blocks away from the street where Taboo, Everly's bookshop, my sister-in-law's boutique, and Montgomery Ink were located. We practically owned that street. However, I had no friends on this street. Just darkness.

"Francesca... Francesca... Oh my God. I remember Francesca. I think."

"Well, she remembers you. Vividly. She gave me some spiel about her former assistant and how she wanted to help, then she couldn't even keep the lies together because suddenly I had to talk to one of my many family members to get the cake for tonight. The cake I'm supposed to have already because I need to get the fucking party together. Why did I think I could surprise my wife? She knows everything. It has taken a colossal effort from every single one of my family members to keep this secret from my wife, and I think she's on to me.

And now I'm not even going to be able to get her a goddamn cake when I know she loves cake."

I was practically screaming now, and people were walking away from me. If I wasn't careful, I was going to get arrested. Great, being behind bars for my wife's surprise party was probably going to be *the icing on the cake I did not have.*

"Calm yourself. Breathe. Okay, Maya currently has Nate, James, and Brooklyn. Therefore, you don't have to deal with them. We've got them until the babysitter comes. Now, do you need me to call Thea? Between Thea and Hailey, you can get a cake done. Or something. I don't know. They're bakers. It's what they do."

I let out a breath. "And another one of our cousins has a sister-in-law that owns a bakery here. We can get it done. Right?"

"We can get it done. Do you want me to handle it?"

I shook my head then realized he couldn't see me. "No, I just needed to yell at you. What did you do?"

"What did I do? She cheated on me with two different guys in my bed. She was the last person I dated before Holly. And when Holly and I didn't work out, I thought that that kind of breakup was a balm on the ache that was the horrendous breakup with Francesca. I never cheated on her, I treated her like a queen, and she stole from me. Did I mention that? She stole from me."

"Why didn't you tell me that when I told you who was baking the cake?" I growled.

"I didn't know it was that Francesca. She never used to bake cakes. At least I don't remember. It's been a long time. Do you remember everyone that you slept with?"

"I think so?"

"The fact that you don't even know tells me that you shouldn't yell at me."

I barked out a laugh. "Okay, I need to go beg family members for some form of cake. And then I need to go home and shower so I can convince my wife to go out for a nice, pleasant dinner with me. And then surprise her and hope she doesn't hate me because she hates surprises."

"She hates surprises?" Jakes asked softly.

"She mentioned once or twice she didn't like surprises, and now that I'm saying it out loud, I'm realizing this is the worst thing I could've done, and now I'm panicking. I am Storm motherfucking Montgomery. I do not panic."

"Hmm, whatever you say. Call me when you need help because I can do that. I can drop everything. I've got you."

"No. I'll handle it."

I hung up and used the time to calm down before I stepped into Taboo, Hailey's bakery.

She gave me one look, her eyes wide. "What is it?"

"I need your help."

"What is it? What can I do?"

"I need a cake."

Hailey dropped her phone, and I caught it before it hit the ground.

"A cake? I thought you were using another person. Not that I blamed you. With everything going on with all of our family members, it made sense you were going to go with an outside company. But what happened?"

I explained, and Hailey's eyes narrowed. "Okay, let me see what I can do. I can talk with Erin, she owns a cake decorating company, but she's slammed with weddings right now."

I shook my head. "I texted her on the way here. She can't even make it to the party tonight with Devin."

Devin was married into the family through the Colorado Springs branch somehow. I tried not to get too complicated with family trees. It hurt my head.

"Oh, I didn't know that. Oh crap. What about Thea? I can do what I can here, but I don't have the capability to make a cake like you're looking for. Not with the number of people coming."

I growled. "I'll see if Thea can help. But we're already so late in the day."

"What about cupcakes?"

I blinked. "Cupcakes?"

"Cupcakes could work. I know it's not a huge cake, but that's something I can do in this kitchen. And if Thea can get up here, we can make this work." She started nodding and took out her phone. "You know what? I got this. You go do everything else that you need to do for the party. I can do the cupcakes."

"Hailey. You can't. I shouldn't have asked you. You've got everything going on."

She gave me a sad smile. "I'm healthy, Storm. I didn't want to stress you out but don't worry. It's not back."

I nearly fell to my knees and let out a breath. "Jesus Christ. Hailey." I hugged her tight and then leaned back as I wiped away her tears.

"Seriously, I'm okay. It really was just the flu. Now, I'm going to bake some cupcakes, and I'm already texting with Thea, and she is in."

"What do you mean she's in?"

"She is packing the car with supplies, and we are going to go cupcake crazy. We physically don't have time to make a full cake, but we can make this work."

"What am I making work?" Sloane asked as he walked in from Montgomery Ink next door. He was Hailey's husband and my good friend.

"My icing king, you have just been drafted into the cupcake business."

"What am I doing, and do I want to know?"

"I'll explain it all. Storm, go get ready for the party. You don't need to worry about this. We're family."

I crushed Hailey to me, kissed the top of her head, gave Sloane an equally hard hug, and ran out of the place, knowing I also needed to deal with the caterer, the bartenders, and everyone else.

Why I'd thought I could do this on my own without my planner siblings and in-laws, I didn't know, but I was going to figure it out.

And apparently, tonight, we were having cupcakes.

Everly

"What are we doing again?" I asked as I slid my hands down my black dress. "Not that I mind going out to dinner with you. It's just we rarely get to go out, just the two of us looking like we do. Seriously though, that suit? You look hot."

Storm gave me a soft smile, though the manic energy radiating off him kind of worried me. In fact, everybody was acting weird. They were all busy with a thousand things and stressed out about something. I didn't know what it was, but I wished they would talk to me.

"I just wanted to spend time with you," he said after a moment before he reached out and squeezed my bare knee.

I shivered, swallowing hard. "If you don't stop touching my knee like that, we're going to have to pull over."

He groaned before letting me go. Not without giving me one last squeeze, though.

I pressed my thighs together and rolled my eyes. "I swear, sometimes it's like we're just dating again, and we aren't the parents of three kids."

"We do okay. Just saying."

"We do, and I'm excited that we get to go up to Fort Collins soon. I miss seeing Clay."

My husband looked over at me and grinned. "We see him often. Same with the kids and Riggs."

"They're still the cutest couple ever. Their wedding was gorgeous. Although watching the kids stand up as Clay's best man and maid of honor just made it all the most special."

"The fact that Clay asked if it was okay that I wasn't his best man just made it the best."

"And our cousins stood up for both him and Riggs. I'm glad that we forced him out of our nest and into the Fort Collins branch."

They had the perfect space for him. He's family.

Clay had been part of Storm's life for longer than I had even known him. Now Clay was an adult, married, with three kids. I still couldn't quite believe that we had three kids of our own, and I'd been married to Storm for long enough that it felt like this was everything my life should have been for ages.

"What restaurant are we going to?"

"You'll see."

I frowned. "You know I don't like surprises."

His hands tightened on the steering wheel, and I frowned, but I didn't say anything. We pulled into a swanky restaurant, and my eyes widened.

"Oh, I love this place. They have the best steak."

"They do," he said as he got out of the car, practically ran around the side, and opened the door for me.

"Why do you seem so nervous? What's going on with you, babe?"

"Nothing. I just love you." He kissed me soundly on the mouth, and I looked up at him, wondering what was up with him.

"Baby, what's wrong?"

"Come on, let's go inside."

"You're shaking, Storm."

"Please, let's just go sit down. We'll get a drink."

"It seems like you need one, okay." I shook my head, laughing as I slid my hand into his. I gripped my clutch as he closed the door behind me, and we made our way inside. The place was quiet, almost too quiet, and I had to wonder if it was even open. There were a few cars in the parking lot, but I hadn't really paid attention to how many. Storm was acting weird enough that I hadn't had a chance to.

"What on earth?" I asked as we walked in, the lights off.

Then the lights turned on quickly, nearly blinding me, and what seemed like a thousand voices shouted. "Surprise!"

I staggered back into Storm, my eyes watering as I put my hand over my face. "Storm!"

"Happy birthday," he whispered as he kissed my cheek. I looked around at all the smiling faces of our friends, family, and everyone that meant so much to me.

Even Clay and Riggs were there, as well as our Fort Collins Montgomery family, and I couldn't help it. I burst into tears, twisted on my heels, and flew into Storm's arms. He wrapped his arms around me and spun me around as people laughed and cheered, then I was on my feet, and Clay and Riggs were moving forward. They handed us each a glass of champagne, each kissed me soundly on the mouth, then did the same to Storm, and I laughed.

"How on earth did you surprise me like this?" I asked.

Clay beamed. "Your husband is a maniacal genius, and we all had to keep a secret from you, and I have no idea how we did it. However, every single child is with babysitters and friends, and we are here, all free from children for the night, and I'm going to party."

I shook my head, and laughed, and looked up at my husband. "Storm?"

"Please tell me you don't mind the surprise. Because I may go have a nervous breakdown if you hate it."

I looked at him then, at the man that had once been my friend, and then my lover, and then my everything, and I went to my tiptoes and kissed him softly. "I love this, I love you, and you are so getting lucky later."

He laughed into my mouth, and we kissed again before I was whisked away by the others.

I hugged every single family member and friend I could possibly see, and could barely contain my love and admiration for each one of them. They were all dressed to the nines, sparkly dresses and suits and ball gowns. Everyone looked as if they had wanted to party like this for forever and now had an excuse to dress up.

Family members from Colorado Springs, and even Tabby's brothers from Pennsylvania were here. I knew it had to be more a coincidence than planning, but I loved it. People who had married into the family through the Gallaghers, and even the Brady brothers up in Boulder were here.

Every single human that could possibly be related to a Montgomery was in this room, and I couldn't help but shake my head and wonder how we weren't bursting the building to its seams. Of course, if we had brought the children, there wouldn't be space at all.

I looked around, then threw my arms around Nessa, my former bookstore employee and good friend. She had an arm around her husband Miles' waist, and I looked at the kids who weren't kids anymore. They had brought their former roommates, who also were seemingly related somehow to the Montgomerys, although that hurt my brain to think about, and I just laughed.

Seriously, every single person I loved, other than the children—who were safe and sound—was in this room.

And when Tabby and my cousin-in-law Thea walked up, I grinned. "Hello, girls."

"Storm, get over here," Thea called, her no-nonsense attitude making me grin. "Okay, we wanted to make sure you saw this before people went at them. I'm not sure we're going to be able to keep them away for long."

I frowned, then looked over at Storm. His eyes were wide, and then I saw what he was staring at.

Cupcakes. So many cupcakes I couldn't even count them all.

"We went a little overboard. But we had help."

"It was fun," a few of the other Montgomerys said, and I could tell they were all hyped up on sugar.

"How did you . . . you did this?" I asked as I wiped tears.

"Storm will tell you the cake story later. However, we told you we weren't going to let you down. We have every kind of sweet cupcake you could ever want, some chocolate, some not, and a couple of savory cupcakes because I've always wanted to try those," Thea added.

I set down my drink, hugged my family, and then threw myself into my husband's arms.

"I love you," he whispered.

"I can't even keep up right now."

"Don't you worry about it. Everyone else will be here in a minute. Let's just breathe, you and me."

And when the music started, and I found myself on the dance floor with my husband, I knew he was right.

Later I would eat a cupcake, indulge in the sweet sensation of my favorite flavors, but first, I would just lean into the man of my life, the man who could surprise me even without trying, and the man who knew everything about me.

My Storm, my Montgomery.

Call Me Cupcake

PB&C Cupcakes (Peanut Butter & Chocolate)

Tiramisu Cupcakes

Banana Split Cupcakes

Peaches and Cream Cupcakes

Steak & Ale Pie

PB&C CUPCAKES
(Peanut Butter & Chocolate)

1 box chocolate cake mix
½ cup butter, softened
1 cup creamy peanut butter
2 cups powdered sugar
3 tablespoons milk
1 teaspoon vanilla extract
2 eggs

Bake cake in cupcake tins according to package directions. To make frosting, combine butter, peanut butter, powdered sugar, milk, and vanilla extract in a large bowl. Allow cakes to cool then spread with icing.

TIRAMISU CUPCAKES

1 box vanilla cake mix
1 (8 ounce) block cream cheese, softened
½ cup powdered sugar
1 teaspoon instant coffee powder
2 tablespoons coffee liqueur
¾ cup heavy cream
1 cup of your favorite coffee
Cocoa powder, for dusting

Bake cupcakes in cupcake tins according to package directions. To make frosting, combine cream cheese, powdered sugar, instant coffee powder, coffee liqueur, and heavy cream in a large bowl. Allow cakes to cool, then dip the tops of each cake into your favorite cup of coffee. Spread frosting on each cake, then dust with cocoa powder.

BANANA SPLIT CUPCAKES

1 box yellow cake mix
1 cup mashed bananas
½ cup vegetable oil
¼ cup water
3 eggs
1 stick (8 tablespoons) butter, softened
4 cups powdered sugar

4 tablespoons milk
2 tablespoons cocoa powder
Food coloring
Chocolate syrup
Maraschino cherries
Sprinkles

Heat oven to 350 degrees. Place baking cups in 12 muffin cups. In a large bowl, mix together cake mix, bananas, oil, water, and eggs. Fill each muffin cup, leaving about ¼-inch headspace. Bake 15-20 minutes or until golden brown. While the cupcakes are cooling, make the frosting. In a small bowl, mix together butter, powdered sugar, and milk until smooth. Distribute into 3 bowls then add food coloring to one bowl to make pink. Add cocoa powder to one bowl, and leave one bowl white. Pipe onto cakes then top with chocolate syrup, cherries and sprinkles.

PEACHES AND CREAM CUPCAKES

1 box vanilla cake mix
¾ cup butter, softened
¾ cup sugar
¾ cup dark brown sugar
2 eggs
1 ½ cups sour cream
4 fresh or canned peaches, diced
1 (8 ounce) block cream cheese
1 stick butter, softened
1 teaspoon vanilla extract
3 cups powdered sugar

Preheat oven to 350 degrees. In a large bowl, combine cake mix, butter, sugar, brown sugar, eggs, sour cream, and peaches until smooth. Fill each muffin cup leaving about ¼-inch headspace. Bake 15-20 minutes or until golden brown. While the cupcakes are cooling, mix together the frosting. In a small bowl, mix together cream cheese, butter, vanilla, and powdered sugar until smooth, then frost each cupcake.

STEAK & ALE PIE

1 pound cubed stew beef

1 sweet onion, diced

1 tablespoon minced garlic

1 can lager beer (I use Michelob Lager)

1 teaspoon dried thyme

2 tablespoons Worcestershire sauce

1 teaspoon salt

2 cups cubed potatoes

1 cup mushrooms, thinly sliced

1 tablespoon cornstarch

2 9-inch pie crusts

In a large saucepan over low heat, add cubed beef, onion, garlic, and beer. Simmer for 30-45 minutes or until beef is tender. Preheat oven to 400 degrees. Add thyme, Worcestershire sauce, salt, potatoes, and mushrooms to the beef, cover and simmer for 10-15 more minutes until the potatoes are tender. In a small bowl, whisk together the cornstarch in ½ cup COLD water. Stir into beef and simmer until slightly thickened. Place one pie crust into a 9-inch pie plate. Spoon beef mixture into pie plate and top with remaining pie crust. Cut small slits in the top for steam to vent and crimp edges with a fork. Bake for 35-40 minutes until crust is golden brown.

CHAPTER 8
Isn't it Sweet

Jillian

And the cake fell. Just like that, it fell. I sighed, leaned against the kitchen island, my butt on the floor, my head resting against the bottom of the granite, and I counted to ten.

This was fine. It wasn't the end of the world. I had tossed a few cakes and desserts in my time. The fact that I wasn't the greatest baker in the world wasn't new. If anything, it was quite blasé that I sucked at baking. But I wanted a cake that was just ours. A cake that was our Montgomery tradition, that wasn't the rest of the large family that I couldn't keep up with. My dad had always baked for me, not well, and sometimes things tasted a little too much like baking powder, but it worked for us.

Now I was a mother of three and worked long hours as a plumber, something that people still gave me the side-eye over because I was "just a woman."

I rolled my eyes at that, annoyed with myself for letting their words influence even my own thoughts.

However, I just had to remind myself that I was fine. That I could do it. I could be a mother, a business owner, a boss. That I could bake a damn cake.

I turned off the oven, pulled out the cake tins, and proceeded to toss their insides into the trash.

"Mom! What are you doing?" Riley, my ten-year-old, ran into the kitchen and frowned. "What happened?"

Addy and Cody followed, six and five, respectively.

"It fell. I don't think I have the measurements quite right, considering nobody was bouncing in here. Therefore, we didn't let it fall because of that."

"We were careful not to come into the kitchen," Cody added as he slid his hand into mine when I stood up.

I looked at my three kids and then held out my free hand. Both Riley and Addy clung to me, and I hugged my babies close, annoyed with myself.

"Okay, let's see what we can do." Addy pulled out my phone, put in the password, and proceeded to search on the internet for different recipes. I rolled my eyes, a little worried that she was better at using the phone than I was, considering I could use a search engine like an expert, but my little girl was proficient at anything that she did. She would probably learn how to bake a cake faster than I did. True, she didn't really have far to go, considering I sucked at it.

"Well, hello there, kids of mine. What are we doing?" Wes asked as he walked in, setting down his electronics: his tablets, phones, and planner. He was up to date on every technological aspect there was out there and was constantly learning how to strategize his days better. The fact that he had only gotten more planner-centric after the kids were born should have annoyed me. Instead, it just endeared him to me more. He was so fricking cute I couldn't stand it.

"The cake didn't make it," Addy said with a prolonged sigh as Cody nodded solemnly.

Riley snapped her fingers. "I think we mixed up the baking powder and the baking soda. But don't worry, we will find an answer." She immediately pulled out a pad and pen and started to write down notes, and I just shook my head, my love for my kids growing with each passing minute.

Wes smiled. "You guys will figure it out. I promise."

"And you're not going to help," I said as I pointed my finger at him.

Wes held up both hands. "I haven't been making any notes. This is all you, baby. I promise."

I cringed. "I know I'm nonsensical. But I can't help it. You're just so good at everything. I mean, the kids are as good as you. Just let me have this one."

"We'll help, Mom, don't worry," Addy said sagely, and I held back a smile.

"You're a menace, and I love you." I kissed her softly on the head, then did to the others, before I went to my husband and held him tight. "So what's the plan tonight?"

Wes grimaced, and I frowned. "What is it?"

"The plan is that Storm is on his way here to watch the kids, and you and I need to go out to the job site."

"What's wrong?" I asked him, alarmed.

"There may be a leak, and I can't figure it out."

"You didn't call or text?" I turned around to Riley, who was handing me my phone without asking. I winked at her and then looked down at my screen. "Seriously, no texts?"

"It's your night off. You're supposed to have the whole weekend. We both are. But I couldn't figure it out, so we need you out there. Since Steve is on vacation, and Star is on maternity leave, I can't ask your team."

I nodded and grimaced. "Okay, I wonder what it could be. It's a new build."

"It's a new build as an addition to an old build. Meaning who knows what could happen."

"And Steve's been off a bit. It's been bugging me," I muttered as Wes nodded.

Steve was a new hire, and he was good, but he tended to miss things, and as a plumber where people relied on you even as they pushed at you, that worried me.

"Let me change, get my gear, then Storm will be here?"

"Yes, and I'm going with you."

"I can do it myself. You could've stayed."

"Think of it as a date."

I laughed. "Yes, a date with plumbing. Sounds great."

"I am sure there are a few jokes I could put there, but I won't."

I shook my head and quickly changed. By the time I was out, Storm was in the kitchen, going over recipe ideas with the kids. "Don't let your uncle help."

"I'm not going to be helping with this. We're going to go through dinner. We both know that I don't deal well with cake right now."

I laughed at the inside joke, and then we made our way to the truck after saying goodbye to the kids.

"You ready?" Wes asked as he hopped into the passenger side of my truck. I nodded, then pulled out of the driveway and headed towards the job site.

"I don't want to have to replace Steve, but if it is a leak on his part, this will be the second time."

"Pretty much, and if there's a leak, that means it could affect other things. You're going to need to hire someone else anyway. You needed to even before Steve's fuck-ups."

"I'll talk with Archer. He might have an idea."

Archer was my counterpart up in Fort Collins and usually had a better lead on people to hire than I did. I didn't know how. The guy was magic.

It took twenty minutes, and then we pulled into the job site, got out, and as soon as I walked in, I knew there was a leak. I couldn't see it. I just felt it in my bones. Call it plumber's intuition. I knew.

"Fuck," I muttered, and I made my way to the section where Steve had been working last.

It took an hour of searching, feeling up drywall, and then of finally tearing it down before I saw the pinprick leak in a pipe that had been newly installed on my day off.

"He shouldn't have missed this."

"Nope. We can give him a 'three strikes, you're out' policy, but this could've been way worse. We weren't finished putting up the walls, and the floors aren't even in yet. But if I hadn't noticed something off before I left today?"

I shuddered to think of it at Wes's words and growled. "Okay, let me get out to my truck to see what I can do to fix this, but then I don't know what to do about Steve."

"More training?" Wes asked.

"Maybe. But he also has an attitude problem, which doesn't help. If he was a nice guy, then that's one thing. But he's a bastard who doesn't like working for women."

"You never told me that," Wes put in, scowling.

"Because I'm used to it."

"I remember what happened the first day that you started working for us. And what those assholes said."

"And you took care of it. Just like I'm taking care of it. Steve isn't outright hostile, not like those guys were. However, I don't know. We're going to wait till he gets back, and I'm going to see what my gut says. But we have enough to fire him, and I totally want to."

"I'm sorry, babe." He leaned forward and kissed me, and I grinned up at him. "Hey, I thought we said no kissing in the workplace."

"It's after hours. If I wanted to fuck you right here on the cement floor, I could."

I rolled my eyes. "Concrete dust in certain areas is not fun. Therefore, I would be riding you."

"Well, I'm sure we can find your kneepads," he added with a wink, and I rolled my eyes before we got to work. Wes was just pulling back another piece of drywall that we'd have to replace when I stopped him, freezing at the sound of something that shouldn't be there.

"What?" he asked. "Is it another snake?"

"No, it was something different. I can't tell what it is." I pulled out my flashlight and blinked. "Oh no."

"What?"

"It seems that the leak has been here for a bit longer than we thought, because there's a hole on the other side of the wall, and somebody left kittens."

"Kittens?" Wes asked, his eyes wide. "What?"

"Kittens, in a box, with a baby blanket, and no mom to be seen. Wes, there's no food left. No water. I think I'm going to cry."

Very carefully, keeping an eye on the kittens, Wes pulled back the rest of the drywall, and I looked down at the four kittens, meowing, and I did my best not to sob.

"They're not bottle-fed anymore. They look to be big enough for wet food." I looked down at the dry paper plate. "They had that. But damn it. Get me my water."

Wes was already pulling it out, pouring it into the cap so the kittens could drink. They started mewing, little cries making my heart hurt. I met Wes's gaze and swallowed hard. "The only vet I know is up in Boulder." I clearly wasn't thinking straight.

"I'm already on it; I'm about to call the emergency vet to get them in."

"Wes, somebody left them here. You don't think it was Steve, do you?"

Wes shook his head. "He's not a horrible person, maybe an asshole, but not a kitten murderer."

I was still crying as the kittens started to crawl on my lap, so I let all four move along my legs. There were two little gray ones, a black-and-white one, and a bright orange one. I didn't know how kitten genetics worked, but they were all about the same size, their eyes were open, and they were mewing for food. I wished I had something for them, but they would have to do with water until we could figure out what to do.

"They can get us in. We've got to go."

"We need to close up. The water's off."

"We'll deal with it in the morning. Hell, I'll call Decker to come out here."

I nodded, and we piled into the truck with the sad little box of kittens between us. They meowed their little kitten squeaks, making my eyes burn.

"How could somebody just do that?"

"I don't want to think about it, babe. But we're here. We got them in time." I had to hope.

I looked down at the little kittens, and all thoughts of asshole plumbers, leaky pipes, and falling cakes fled. Kittens, like my babies, tended to wrap their way around my heart, and I honestly didn't know what I would do if something happened to any of them.

Wes

Two hours later, the kittens were given a full checkup and were in perfect health. A little hungry, but apparently, they seemed to have only run out of food that morning. They were slightly dehydrated but didn't need subcutaneous fluids. And they were adorable. They were too small for a chip and so cute that I couldn't help but watch Jillian fall all over them.

"We don't have space here for them, unfortunately," the vet was saying.

I nodded tightly. "Yeah, you guys look full up." My words weren't sarcastic in the least. Every single spot in the place was full of neglected animals, and some very cared-for animals that were here at their owners' request.

"There's a shelter a couple of miles south from us, but they're full as well. So many pets are out there, and these are abandoned or from a feral litter. We're so sorry. I can't even take them home right now because I have a set of kittens I'm fostering."

I looked at Jillian, who gave me a slight nod. I let out a breath. "We can take them home."

The vet's eyes widened. "That's amazing, that's four kittens. I have a few questions first, however. Do you have any pets?"

I shook my head. "No, but we have fostered kittens and bottle-fed them before. They ended up going to a family that could handle the pets at the time. We had an infant, so it didn't work out."

We went through the paperwork, and somehow I found myself in a truck with four kittens, an expensive bag of food, a couple of toys, and a small scratching post.

"What are we doing?" I asked.

"All I wanted was cake, and now I have kittens."

"Are we keeping them?" I asked softly before we pulled into the neighborhood. "Because we need to be able to tell the kids that these are only for a couple of nights."

"We already talked with the vet. They said they were ours if we wanted. No wait times with the lack of space and no fosters out there. They could be ours; we just need to come in for checkups and shots."

"That's four. Not one, not two, not three—four kittens. That's more than we have kids."

"Well, we know the kids aren't allergic, neither are we. We can make this work."

"Kittens."

One kitten meowed up at me, and I nodded. "Yes, you."

Jillian's smile was so bright, I couldn't help but fall in love with her all over again.

"Babe."

"I know this isn't neat and orderly and doesn't fit in your plan, and we're going to have to deal with a new hire and possibly firing Steve, as well as the leak that Decker's working on right now, and other things, but I don't know, I think we need these kittens. We can name them after desserts or something. What do you think?"

"Desserts?"

"What? Let's see: Cupcake, Sundae, Parfait, Brûlée—"

"Not Brûlée."

She laughed. "I don't know. We'll think of cute little names for them."

"I'm sure the kids will have a blast doing it. Damn it. It looks like we have four kittens."

Jillian shook her head. "I can't believe I agree with you."

"I think it was your idea."

"I think it was the kittens' idea."

As soon as we pulled into the driveway—I had already texted Storm to warn him—we got out, and we left some of the cat toys and things inside the truck. That way, we could surprise the kids with the box of kittens.

When Storm opened the door for us, his eyes widened, and he shook his head. "You don't do things in half measures, do you?"

"Never," Jillian said with a grin.

I shook my head at the connection between the two since they were best friends, even if they had once dated, and I moved into the house, the box in my hands.

"The kids are in the living room; I said you'd be in there in a minute. That's why they're not meeting you here."

I nodded, handed over the two gray kittens to Jillian as I took the other two in my hands. They rubbed at my beard and then tried to crawl all over my arms. They didn't look scared in the least. They looked excited to be here, as if they had been here all along.

"Holy hell, man."

"Yes."

Storm pulled out his phone. "I'm going to take some photos. Then I'll get whatever you need out of the truck. We've got you."

"I hope so. Because I think we've lost our minds."

Storm just grinned, and then Jillian and I walked into the living room. Riley saw us first, and her eyes widened before she stood up, her hands over her mouth as a squeaking sound slipped through.

Addy and Cody both looked up at that point before Cody threw his hands up in the air and shouted, and Addy began to cry.

"Well, that's one way to react," Storm muttered behind us, laughing even though he was still recording on his phone. He had taken my phone out of my pocket and was snapping photos as well. We had done this before.

"Kids, at the job site, we found some babies that need our help. What do you say to helping out?" Jillian asked.

"Like the fosters. When do we have to give them back?" Riley asked, her voice soft.

I had hated breaking my daughter's heart by having to give the kittens back once we were done fostering. However, the look of hope in her gaze, the hope she tried to hide, cemented this decision in stone. I met Jillian's gaze, and then we both shook our heads.

"No, these are ours to keep. We're going to need help with names." I cleared my throat. "Your mom wants to name them after desserts."

"Trifle!" Riley said. "One of them has to be Trifle."

Storm burst out laughing, and then we were on the ground, kids and kittens all over us, and I knew that this was crazy, that this made no sense, and yet here we were, parents with three kids, four kittens, and a twin brother who was laughing so hard he could barely keep the phone up as he took photos.

I looked at my family, at the kids I couldn't help but love, and the kittens that were going to tear up my house and bury deep in my heart, and I knew that this was the right decision. The craziest one I had ever made, second to falling for the one woman that I shouldn't.

However, we were Montgomerys. We made those choices that no one else would make. We fell hard. We loved hard. And we were forever.

And in the end, that's all that mattered.

Isn't It Sweet

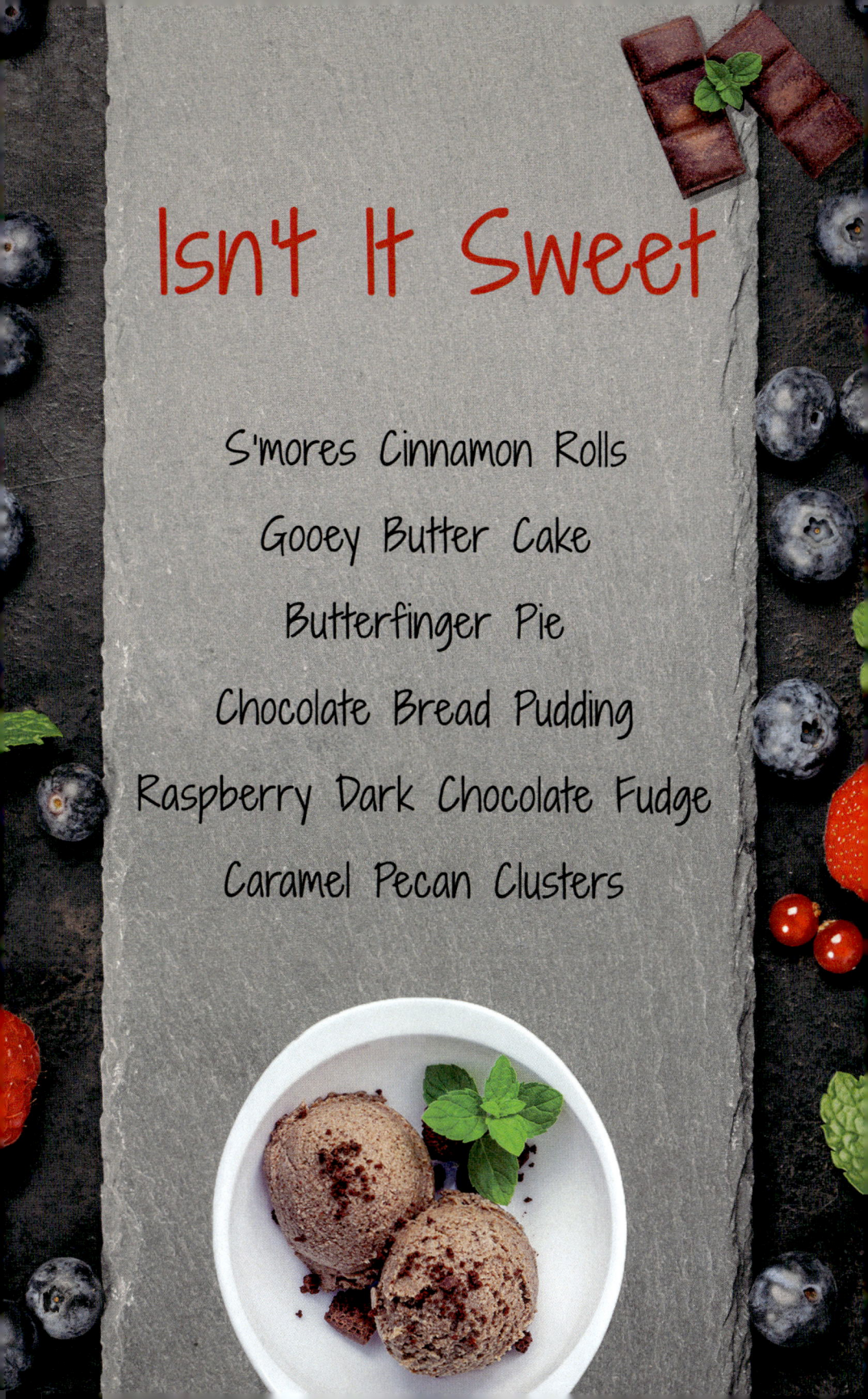

S'mores Cinnamon Rolls

Gooey Butter Cake

Butterfinger Pie

Chocolate Bread Pudding

Raspberry Dark Chocolate Fudge

Caramel Pecan Clusters

S'MORES CINNAMON ROLLS

1 package refrigerated pizza crust
¼ cup Nutella
2 tablespoons butter, melted
¼ cup white sugar
¼ cup brown sugar
1 tablespoon ground cinnamon
1 cup mini marshmallows
¼ cup graham cracker crumbs

Preheat oven to 375 degrees. Unroll pizza crust and spread evenly with Nutella and melted butter, in that order. Sprinkle sugar, brown sugar, cinnamon and marshmallows evenly across all of the dough. Roll up dough lengthwise and slice into 1-inch thick rolls. Place on a greased 9 x 9-inch pan and bake for 15 minutes. Place Cream Cheese Icing in a resealable bag, cut one corner, and pipe onto cinnamon rolls. Sprinkle the rolls with graham cracker crumbs.

Cream Cheese Icing

1 stick butter, softened
1 (8 ounce) block cream cheese
1 teaspoon vanilla extract
3 cups powdered sugar

In a large bowl, using a hand mixer, combine butter, cream cheese, and vanilla until blended. Add powdered sugar one cup at a time until all 3 cups are blended.

GOOEY BUTTER CAKE

1 box yellow cake mix
½ cup (1 stick) butter, melted
2 teaspoons vanilla extract
4 eggs
1 (8 ounce) block cream cheese
4 cups powdered sugar

Preheat oven to 350 degrees. In a large bowl, mix together cake mix, butter, 1 teaspoon vanilla extract, and 2 eggs. Spread into a 9 x 13-inch baking dish. In a separate large bowl using an electric mixer, mix together cream cheese, 2 eggs, and remaining 1 teaspoon vanilla extract, then slowly add in powdered sugar. Pour over cake batter. Bake for 45 minutes. Cool before slicing into squares.

BUTTERFINGER PIE

4 ounces cream cheese, softened
1/3 cup creamy peanut butter
½ cup powdered sugar
2 containers frozen whipped topping, thawed
1 graham cracker crust
2 Butterfinger candy bars, chopped

In a large bowl using a hand mixer, blend together cream cheese, peanut butter, powdered sugar, and 1 ½ containers of whipped topping. Spread into pie crust and top with remaining whipped topping. Sprinkle Butterfinger bits over the top of the pie.

CHOCOLATE BREAD PUDDING

5 eggs
2 ½ cups milk
1 cup dark brown sugar
1 teaspoon cinnamon
1 teaspoon vanilla extract
1 loaf day-old bread, cut into 1-inch cubes
8 ounces milk chocolate chips

Preheat oven to 350 degrees. In a large bowl, mix together eggs, milk, brown sugar, cinnamon, and vanilla extract. Place bread cubes in a greased 9 x 13-inch baking dish. Pour egg mixture over bread and press down to soak the bread in the egg mixture. Sprinkle chocolate chips over the bread pudding. Bake for 1 hour. Serve warm.

RASPBERRY DARK CHOCOLATE FUDGE

10 dark chocolate candy bars (I use Hershey's Special Dark)
1 cup sweetened condensed milk
2 teaspoons raspberry extract

Line an 8-inch square pan with parchment paper. Break the chocolate into small pieces and place in a microwavable bowl. Add sweetened condensed milk and microwave for 30 seconds, then stir and microwave for an additional 30 seconds. Stir until smooth. Mix in raspberry extract and pour into 8-inch pan. Refrigerate for 3-4 hours until set. Cut into 1-inch squares.

CARAMEL PECAN CLUSTERS

8 ounces caramels
2 tablespoons heavy cream
1 teaspoon vanilla extract
2 cups pecans, chopped
½ cup semi-sweet chocolate chips
2 teaspoons vegetable oil

Line a cookie sheet with parchment paper. In a medium saucepan over low heat, combine caramels and heavy cream. Stir until all caramels are melted then remove from heat. Stir in vanilla extract and pecans until all pecans are coated. Spray a small cookie scoop or two small spoons with nonstick spray and scoop the caramel pecan mixture onto the parchment paper. Repeat with remaining mixture. In a microwave safe bowl combine the chocolate chips and oil together. Microwave for 30-45 seconds and stir until smooth. Drizzle the melted chocolate onto each cluster.

Index

Appetizers and Sides

Blue Cheese Chicken Bites 15
Broccoli Cheese Soup 83
Buffalo Chicken Stuffed Bread 40
Cheeseburger Spring Rolls 64
Dirty Martini Deviled Eggs 14
Loaded Potato Dip 14
Eggroll Lettuce Wraps 70
Fried Cheese Curds 82
Jarcuterie Cups 13
S'mores Cinnamon Rolls 108
Smoked Maple Bacon 15
Spicy Corn Chowder 42
Spicy Pop Tarts 68

Main Dishes

3-Cheese Hashbrown Casserole 82
Beef Curry Stir Fry 43
Bold Burger 30
Cajun Chicken Pasta Alfredo 26
Cheesesteak Stuffed Peppers 69
Cheesy Chicken Enchiladas 80
Chili Cheese Waffles 66
French Dip Au Jus 29
French Toast Grilled Cheese with Bacon 81
Memphis Chicken 44

Orange Chicken	28
Peach Pepper Jelly Grilled Chicken	41
Reuben Quesadillas	65
Steak & Ale Pie	98
Steak and Cheddar Melt	84
Tuscan Portobellos	53
Veggie Lasagna	52
Whiskey Honey Ribs	27
Zesty Meatballs	12

Salads

Green Goddess Salad	54
Southwest Pasta Salad	54

Desserts

Banana Split Cupcakes	96
Butterfinger Pie	109
Caramel Pecan Clusters	11
Chocolate Bread Pudding	110
Gooey Butter Cake	109
PB&C Cupcakes (Peanut Butter & Chocolate)	94
Peaches and Cream Cupcakes	97
Raspberry Dark Chocolate Fudge	110
Tiramisu Cupcakes	95

ALSO FROM CARRIE ANN RYAN

The Montgomery Ink: Fort Collins Series:
Book 1: *Inked Persuasion*
Book 2: *Inked Obsession*
Book 3: *Inked Devotion*
Book 3.5: *Nothing But Ink*
Book 4: *Inked Craving*
Book 5: *Inked Temptation*

The Montgomery Ink Legacy Series:
Book 1: *Bittersweet Promises*

The Wilder Brothers Series:
Book 1: *One Way Back to Me*
Book 2: *Always the One for Me*

The Aspen Pack Series:
Book 1: *Etched in Honor*

Montgomery Ink:
Book 0.5: *Ink Inspired*
Book 0.6: *Ink Reunited*
Book 1: *Delicate Ink*
Book 1.5: *Forever Ink*
Book 2: *Tempting Boundaries*
Book 3: *Harder than Words*
Book 3.5: *Finally Found You*
Book 4: *Written in Ink*
Book 4.5: *Hidden Ink*
Book 5: *Ink Enduring*
Book 6: *Ink Exposed*
Book 6.5: *Adoring Ink*

Book 6.6: *Love, Honor, & Ink*
Book 7: *Inked Expressions*
Book 7.3: *Dropout*
Book 7.5: *Executive Ink*
Book 8: *Inked Memories*
Book 8.5: *Inked Nights*
Book 8.7: *Second Chance Ink*

MONTGOMERY INK: COLORADO SPRINGS
Book 1: *Fallen Ink*
Book 2: *Restless Ink*
Book 2.5: *Ashes to Ink*
Book 3: *Jagged Ink*
Book 3.5: *Ink by Numbers*

THE MONTGOMERY INK: BOULDER SERIES:
Book 1: *Wrapped in Ink*
Book 2: *Sated in Ink*
Book 3: *Embraced in Ink*
Book 4: *Seduced in Ink*
Book 4.5: *Captured in Ink*

THE GALLAGHER BROTHERS SERIES:
Book 1: *Love Restored*
Book 2: *Passion Restored*
Book 3: *Hope Restored*

THE WHISKEY AND LIES SERIES:
Book 1: *Whiskey Secrets*
Book 2: *Whiskey Reveals*
Book 3: *Whiskey Undone*

The Fractured Connections Series:
Book 1: *Breaking Without You*
Book 2: *Shouldn't Have You*
Book 3: *Falling With You*
Book 4: *Taken With You*

The Less Than Series:
Book 1: *Breathless With Her*
Book 2: *Reckless With You*
Book 3: *Shameless With Him*

The Promise Me Series:
Book 1: *Forever Only Once*
Book 2: *From That Moment*
Book 3: *Far From Destined*
Book 4: *From Our First*

The On My Own Series:
Book 1: *My One Night*
Book 2: *My Rebound*
Book 3: *My Next Play*
Book 4: *My Bad Decisions*

The Ravenwood Coven Series:
Book 1: *Dawn Unearthed*
Book 2: *Dusk Unveiled*
Book 3: *Evernight Unleashed*

Redwood Pack Series:
Book 1: *An Alpha's Path*
Book 2: *A Taste for a Mate*
Book 3: *Trinity Bound*
Book 3.5: *A Night Away*
Book 4: *Enforcer's Redemption*

Book 4.5: *Blurred Expectations*
Book 4.7: *Forgiveness*
Book 5: *Shattered Emotions*
Book 6: *Hidden Destiny*
Book 6.5: *A Beta's Haven*
Book 7: *Fighting Fate*
Book 7.5: *Loving the Omega*
Book 7.7: *The Hunted Heart*
Book 8: *Wicked Wolf*

THE TALON PACK:
Book 1: *Tattered Loyalties*
Book 2: *An Alpha's Choice*
Book 3: *Mated in Mist*
Book 4: *Wolf Betrayed*
Book 5: *Fractured Silence*
Book 6: *Destiny Disgraced*
Book 7: *Eternal Mourning*
Book 8: *Strength Enduring*
Book 9: *Forever Broken*
Book 10: *Mated in Darkness*

THE ELEMENTS OF FIVE SERIES:
Book 1: *From Breath and Ruin*
Book 2: *From Flame and Ash*
Book 3: *From Spirit and Binding*
Book 4: *From Shadow and Silence*

THE BRANDED PACK SERIES:
(Written with Alexandra Ivy)
Book 1: *Stolen and Forgiven*
Book 2: *Abandoned and Unseen*
Book 3: *Buried and Shadowed*

DANTE'S CIRCLE SERIES:
Book 1: *Dust of My Wings*
Book 2: *Her Warriors' Three Wishes*
Book 3: *An Unlucky Moon*
Book 3.5: *His Choice*
Book 4: *Tangled Innocence*
Book 5: *Fierce Enchantment*
Book 6: *An Immortal's Song*
Book 7: *Prowled Darkness*
Book 8: *Dante's Circle Reborn*

HOLIDAY, MONTANA SERIES:
Book 1: *Charmed Spirits*
Book 2: *Santa's Executive*
Book 3: *Finding Abigail*
Book 4: *Her Lucky Love*
Book 5: *Dreams of Ivory*

THE TATTERED ROYALS SERIES:
Book 1: *Royal Line*
Book 2: *Enemy Heir*

THE HAPPY EVER AFTER SERIES:
Flame and Ink
Ink Ever After

ABOUT CARRIE ANN RYAN

Carrie Ann Ryan is the *New York Times* and *USA Today* bestselling author of contemporary, paranormal, and young adult romance. Her works include the Montgomery Ink, Talon Pack, Promise Me, and Elements of Five series, which have sold millions of books worldwide. She's the winner of an RT Book of the Year and a Prism Award in her genres. She started writing while in graduate school for her advanced degree in chemistry and hasn't stopped since. Carrie Ann has written over seventy-five novels and novellas with more in the works. When she's not losing herself in her emotional and action-packed worlds, she's reading as much as she can while wrangling her clowder of cats who have more followers than she does.

Connect with Carrie Ann

WEBSITE
www.carrieannryan.com

FACEBOOK
www.facebook.com/CarrieAnnRyanAuthor

INSTAGRAM
www.instagram.com/carrieannryanauthor

TIKTOK
www.tiktok.com/@carrieannryan

ALSO FROM SUZANNE M. JOHNSON

Southern Bits & Bites
Southern Kid Bits & Mom Bites
Southern Bits & Bites: Our 150 Favorite Recipes

Writing with Lexi Blake
Master Bits & Mercenary Bites
Master Bits & Mercenary Bites~Girls Night

Writing with J. Kenner
Bar Bites: A Man of the Month Cookbook

Writing with Kristen Proby
Indulge With Me: A With Me in Seattle Celebration

Writing with Larissa Ione
Dining with Angels: Bits & Bites from the Demonica Universe

Writing with Kristen Ashley
Dream Bites Cookbook: Cooking with the Commandos

Writing with Lorelei James
Cowboy Bites: A Rough Riders Cookbook

ABOUT SUZANNE M. JOHNSON

Suzanne Johnson is the *USA Today* bestselling author of three cookbooks, and the recipe developer for six other books with: Lexi Blake, J. Kenner, Kristen Proby, Larissa Ione, and Kristen Ashley. A family-trained South Georgia chef, Suzanne has been cooking all her life, creating not only unique food, but precious memories of meals shared with family and friends. In all her books, Suzanne shows that making delicious meals doesn't have to be complicated—they just have to be made with love.

Connect with Suzanne M. Johnson

WEBSITE
www.southernbitsandbites.com

FACEBOOK
www.facebook.com/Southern-Bits-Bites-352580344928317

INSTAGRAM
southernbitsand_bites

Made in the USA
Las Vegas, NV
02 April 2023